RANJOT SINGH CHAHAL

How to Speak Workplace English with Confidence

Mastering Communication Skills for Professional Success

First published by Rana Books 2024

Copyright © 2024 by Ranjot Singh Chahal

All rights reserved. No part of this publication may be reproduced, stored or transmitted in any form or by any means, electronic, mechanical, photocopying, recording, scanning, or otherwise without written permission from the publisher. It is illegal to copy this book, post it to a website, or distribute it by any other means without permission.

First edition

Contents

1	Introduction	1
2	The Importance of Effective Communication in the Workplace	3
3	Understanding Common Workplace Vocabulary and Phrases	16
4	Tips for Building Confidence in Speaking English at Work	44
5	Navigating Cultural Differences in Communication	63
6	Polite and Professional Language in the Office	73
7	Handling Common Workplace Situations	85
8	Using Email and Written Communication Effectively	93
9	Practicing English Conversations at Work	100
10	Overcoming Communication Challenges	109
11	Building Connections and Networking in English	113

1

Introduction

Welcome to "How to Speak Workplace English with Confidence: Mastering Communication Skills for Professional Success."

In today's dynamic and interconnected global marketplace, proficiency in English communication is crucial for navigating the complexities of the modern workplace. Whether you're communicating with colleagues, clients, or stakeholders, your ability to express yourself effectively in English can significantly impact your professional success.

This book is designed as a comprehensive guide to help you develop and refine your workplace English skills, enabling you to communicate with confidence and clarity in various professional contexts. Whether you're a non-native English speaker seeking to enhance your language proficiency or a seasoned professional aiming to sharpen your communication skills, the strategies and insights offered in this book are tailored to meet your needs.

Each chapter is crafted to address key aspects of workplace communication, from understanding common vocabulary and phrases to mastering email etiquette, navigating cultural nuances, and building professional connections. Through practical tips, real-world examples, and interactive exercises, you'll gain the tools and confidence needed to thrive in any professional environment.

By investing in your English communication skills, you're investing in your future success. So let's embark on this journey together, as we explore the art of speaking workplace English with confidence and paving the way for your professional advancement.

2

The Importance of Effective Communication in the Workplace

Communication is the backbone of any successful organization. It is the key to effective leadership, collaboration, innovation, and overall business success. In the fast-paced and interconnected world of today, effective communication in the workplace is more important than ever before. Whether it's conveying a vision, sharing feedback, resolving conflicts, or building relationships, strong communication skills are essential at every level of an organization.

Effective communication in the workplace encompasses verbal, non-verbal, and written interactions between employees, managers, and other stakeholders. It is about transmitting information clearly, accurately, and timely to ensure that everyone is on the same page and working towards common goals. When communication breaks down, it can lead to misunderstandings, decreased productivity, low morale, and ultimately, hinder the organization's success.

1. Importance of Effective Communication in the Workplace

Effective communication is critical for a variety of reasons. It is the foundation for building strong relationships, fostering trust, and creating a positive work environment. When employees feel heard, understood, and valued, they are more engaged, motivated, and productive. Effective communication also plays a crucial role in enhancing collaboration, problem-solving, and decision-making processes within an organization.

- Enhanced Productivity: Clear and concise communication ensures that tasks are understood correctly, deadlines are met, and resources are allocated efficiently. When instructions are conveyed effectively, employees are better equipped to perform their jobs accurately and efficiently, leading to improved productivity.

- Improved Employee Morale: Open and transparent communication promotes a positive work culture where employees feel empowered, respected, and appreciated. When leaders communicate openly and honestly, it creates a sense of trust and loyalty among team members, boosting morale and job satisfaction.

- Conflict Resolution: Effective communication is essential for resolving conflicts and misunderstandings in the workplace. By encouraging open dialogue and active listening, employees can address differences constructively, find common ground, and work towards mutually beneficial solutions.

- Better Decision-Making: Clear communication ensures that

all relevant information is shared, discussed, and understood before making decisions. When team members communicate effectively, they can consider different perspectives, weigh options, and make informed decisions that benefit the organization as a whole.

2. Types of Communication in the Workplace

Effective communication in the workplace can take various forms, including verbal, non-verbal, and written communication. Each type of communication serves a different purpose and plays a unique role in conveying information, building relationships, and achieving organizational goals.

- Verbal Communication: Verbal communication involves speaking and listening to convey messages. It can take place in various settings, such as team meetings, one-on-one discussions, presentations, or informal conversations. Verbal communication is essential for clarifying instructions, discussing ideas, providing feedback, and engaging with colleagues.

Example: A manager holds a team meeting to discuss upcoming projects and assigns tasks to team members based on their expertise and availability. During the meeting, team members have the opportunity to ask questions, seek clarification, and provide input on the project's goals and requirements.

- Non-Verbal Communication: Non-verbal communication includes gestures, facial expressions, body language, and tone of voice. It plays a significant role in conveying emotions, attitudes, and intentions without using words. Non-verbal cues can complement verbal messages and provide additional context to enhance understanding.

Example: During a performance review, an employee sits upright, makes eye contact, nods in agreement, and smiles when receiving positive feedback from their manager. These non-verbal cues indicate that the employee is engaged, receptive, and appreciative of the feedback provided.

- Written Communication: Written communication involves conveying information through written documents, emails, reports, memos, and other forms of written correspondence. It is essential for documenting information, sharing updates, providing instructions, and maintaining a record of communications within the organization.

Example: An employee sends an email to their colleagues detailing the key points discussed in a recent meeting, including action items, deadlines, and responsibilities. The written communication serves as a reference guide for team members to stay informed and aligned on the project's progress.

3. Benefits of Effective Communication in the Workplace

Effective communication in the workplace offers numerous benefits that contribute to the organization's success, employee satisfaction, and overall performance. By fostering a culture of open communication, organizations can create a positive work environment where employees feel motivated, engaged, and connected to their colleagues and the company's mission.

- Increased Employee Engagement: Clear communication helps employees understand their roles, responsibilities, and expectations within the organization. When employees are well-informed and involved in decision-making processes, they feel more engaged, motivated, and committed to achieving common goals.

Example: A company introduces a new employee feedback system where employees can share their ideas, concerns, and suggestions with upper management. By actively listening to employees' feedback and implementing relevant suggestions, the company demonstrates a commitment to engaging employees in shaping the organization's culture and practices.

- Stronger Team Collaboration: Effective communication promotes collaboration among team members by fostering trust, transparency, and mutual respect. When team members communicate openly, share information, and collaborate on tasks, they can leverage their diverse skills and perspectives to achieve shared objectives.

Example: A cross-functional team works on a project that requires close collaboration between departments. By communicating regularly, sharing updates, and addressing challenges collectively, team members can leverage their expertise and work together efficiently to deliver high-quality results.

- Improved Customer Relationships: Clear and effective communication with customers is vital for building strong relationships, meeting their needs, and enhancing customer satisfaction. When employees communicate professionally, empathetically, and responsively with customers, it creates a positive impression and fosters long-term loyalty.

Example: A customer service representative communicates with a dissatisfied customer who encountered an issue with a product. By actively listening to the customer's concerns, offering solutions, and following up to ensure resolution, the representative demonstrates a commitment to providing excellent customer service and building trust with the customer.

- Enhanced Innovation and Creativity: Effective communication stimulates creativity and innovation within the organization by encouraging employees to share ideas, think critically, and explore new solutions to challenges. When employees feel safe to express their thoughts and opinions, it fosters a culture of innovation that drives continuous improvement and growth.

Example: An organization implements a weekly innovation challenge where employees are encouraged to submit creative ideas to improve processes, products, or services. By promoting a culture of open communication and idea-sharing, the organization creates opportunities for employees to contribute to the company's innovation efforts and drive positive change.

4. Challenges in Communication in the Workplace

Despite its importance, effective communication in the workplace can face various challenges that hinder clarity, understanding, and alignment among employees. Identifying and addressing these challenges is essential for overcoming communication barriers and fostering a culture of effective communication within the organization.

- Misinterpretation and Misunderstanding: Misinterpretation and misunderstanding can occur when messages are unclear, ambiguous, or open to interpretation. Differences in communication styles, cultural backgrounds, or language proficiency can contribute to miscommunication and lead to confusion or conflicts.

Example: During a team meeting, a manager uses technical jargon and complex terminology that some team members may not fully understand. As a result, team members may misinterpret the manager's instructions or recommendations, leading to errors or delays in project implementation.

- Information Overload: In today's digital age, employees are often bombarded with a constant stream of emails, messages, notifications, and updates. Information overload can overwhelm employees, making it challenging to prioritize important communications, stay focused, and digest critical information effectively.

Example: An employee receives multiple emails, instant messages, and notifications throughout the day, making it difficult to keep track of essential tasks, deadlines, or updates. As a result, the employee may struggle to manage their workload efficiently and may miss important communication that requires immediate attention.

- Hierarchical Communication: Hierarchical communication structures can hinder open dialogue, feedback, and collaboration among employees at different levels of the organization. When communication flows strictly from top to bottom or vice versa, it can create barriers to sharing diverse perspectives, innovative ideas, and constructive feedback.

Example: In a hierarchical organization, lower-level employees may feel reluctant to share their ideas, concerns, or feedback with senior management due to perceived power differentials or fear of repercussions. As a result, valuable insights and perspectives from frontline employees may go unheard, limiting the organization's ability to innovate and adapt to change.

5. Strategies for Improving Communication in the Workplace

Overcoming communication challenges and fostering a culture of effective communication requires proactive strategies, tools, and practices that promote clarity, transparency, and engagement among employees. By implementing these strategies, organizations can enhance communication skills, build stronger relationships, and drive performance and innovation.

- Promote Active Listening: Encouraging active listening is essential for fostering understanding, empathy, and collaboration among team members. By actively listening to others, employees demonstrate respect, validate perspectives, and create space for open dialogue and meaningful exchanges.

Example: During a team meeting, team members practice active listening by maintaining eye contact, nodding in agreement, and summarizing key points to demonstrate understanding. By listening attentively to their colleagues' ideas, concerns, and feedback, team members build trust, foster mutual respect, and encourage open communication within the team.

- Provide Constructive Feedback: Offering constructive feedback is crucial for promoting professional growth, development, and performance improvement within the organization. When managers and colleagues provide timely, specific, and actionable feedback, employees can learn from their experiences, address areas for improvement, and enhance their skills and competencies.

Example: A manager provides constructive feedback to an employee on their presentation skills, highlighting areas of strength and opportunities for improvement. By offering specific examples, actionable suggestions, and support for skill development, the manager equips the employee with the guidance needed to enhance their presentation abilities and excel in future presentations.

- Use Multiple Communication Channels: Leveraging different communication channels, such as face-to-face meetings, video conferences, emails, instant messaging, and collaboration tools, allows employees to choose the most effective channel for conveying messages, sharing updates, and collaborating on tasks. By using a variety of communication channels, organizations can enhance flexibility, accessibility, and responsiveness in communication practices.

Example: A project team communicates using a combination of face-to-face meetings, virtual video conferences, and instant messaging platforms to discuss project progress, share updates, and address critical issues. By utilizing multiple communication channels, team members can stay connected, collaborate effectively, and adapt to changing communication needs based on the nature of the project and its requirements.

- Encourage Open Communication: Creating a culture of open communication involves promoting transparency, honesty, and inclusivity within the organization. Encouraging employees to share their thoughts, ideas, and concerns openly without fear of judgment or reprisal fosters a work environment where diverse perspectives are valued, and meaningful conversations can take place.

Example: A company establishes an open-door policy where employees are encouraged to approach their managers, colleagues, or HR representatives to discuss any concerns, feedback, or suggestions they may have. By fostering a culture of open communication and active listening, the company demonstrates a commitment to valuing employees' voices and promoting a supportive work environment where open dialogue is welcome and encouraged.

6. Tools and Technologies for Enhancing Communication in the Workplace

In today's digital age, advancements in technology have revolutionized the way organizations communicate, collaborate, and engage with employees. Leveraging tools and technologies that enable seamless communication, information sharing, and collaboration can enhance productivity, efficiency, and effectiveness in the workplace.

- Collaboration Platforms: Collaboration platforms, such as Microsoft Teams, Slack, and Google Workspace, allow employees to communicate, share files, and collaborate on projects in real time. These platforms offer features like instant messaging, video conferencing, document sharing, and project management tools that facilitate effective communication and collaboration among remote and distributed teams.

Example: A remote team uses Slack to communicate, share updates, and collaborate on a project in real time. Team members can create dedicated channels for different topics, share files, and integrate third-party apps to streamline communication and productivity. By leveraging collaboration platforms, the team can stay connected, aligned, and productive regardless of their physical location.

- Project Management Tools: Project management tools, such as Asana, Trello, and Jira, help teams plan, track, and manage projects efficiently by organizing tasks, setting deadlines, and assigning responsibilities. These tools offer features like task lists, kanban boards, and Gantt charts that enable teams to coordinate work, communicate progress, and collaborate effectively on complex projects.

Example: A project team uses Asana to track project milestones, assign tasks, and monitor progress throughout the project lifecycle. Team members can set deadlines, update task statuses, and communicate with colleagues within the platform to ensure that everyone is aligned and informed on project timelines and deliverables. By utilizing project management tools, the team can streamline communication, collaboration, and project execution to achieve project goals successfully.

- Feedback and Survey Tools: Feedback and survey tools, such as SurveyMonkey, Typeform, and Google Forms, enable organizations to collect feedback, opinions, and insights from employees on various topics, including job satisfaction, training needs, and organizational culture. These tools facilitate data collection, analysis, and reporting to inform decision-making and drive continuous improvement in communication practices.

Example: An organization distributes a feedback survey to employees to gather input on their communication preferences, challenges, and suggestions for improvement. By collecting anonymous feedback through a survey tool, the organization can identify trends, opportunities, and areas for enhancement in communication strategies and practices. Using feedback and survey tools enables organizations to engage employees, solicit input, and enhance communication effectiveness based on actionable insights.

7. Conclusion

In conclusion, effective communication is the cornerstone of success in the workplace. It underpins collaboration, innovation, employee engagement, and organizational performance. By fostering a culture of open communication, active listening, and transparency, organizations can create a positive work environment where employees feel valued, respected, and motivated to contribute their best work.

The importance of effective communication in the workplace

cannot be overstated. It is essential for building strong relationships, resolving conflicts, making informed decisions, and achieving shared goals. By recognizing the significance of effective communication and implementing strategies to overcome communication challenges, organizations can unlock the full potential of their employees, drive performance, and thrive in today's dynamic and competitive business environment.

As technology continues to evolve, organizations have more tools and resources at their disposal to enhance communication, collaboration, and engagement among employees. By leveraging communication tools and technologies strategically, organizations can streamline workflows, facilitate information sharing, and empower employees to communicate effectively across different channels and platforms.

Ultimately, effective communication in the workplace is a catalyst for organizational success and growth. It enables employees to connect, collaborate, and innovate, driving performance and achieving strategic objectives. By prioritizing effective communication as a core value and integrating communication best practices into everyday interactions, organizations can build a strong foundation for sustained success, resilience, and competitiveness in the ever-changing business landscape.

3

Understanding Common Workplace Vocabulary and Phrases

Understanding common workplace vocabulary and phrases is essential for effective communication and collaboration in professional environments. Whether you are a seasoned employee or a new hire, having a good grasp of workplace jargon can help you navigate conversations, meetings, and projects more confidently. In this comprehensive guide, we will delve deep into various common workplace vocabulary and phrases, providing explanations, examples, and contexts to help you gain a better understanding.

1. General Workplace Vocabulary:

a) Deadline: A deadline is a specific time or date by which a task or project must be completed. It is crucial to meet deadlines to ensure the smooth functioning of the organization and project timelines. Example: "We need to finish the report by Friday; that's our deadline."

b) Multitasking: Multitasking refers to the ability to perform multiple tasks or activities simultaneously. It is a valuable skill in the workplace, but it is essential to prioritize tasks effectively. Example: "She is great at multitasking; she can handle emails, calls, and meetings all at once."

c) Collaboration: Collaboration entails working together with others to achieve a common goal or complete a project. Effective collaboration involves communication, sharing resources, and leveraging diverse skills. Example: "The team collaborated on the presentation, combining their expertise for a successful outcome."

d) Feedback: Feedback is information provided to individuals about their performance, behavior, or work. Constructive feedback is key to personal and professional growth. Example: "I appreciate your feedback on my presentation; I will work on improving my public speaking skills."

e) Leadership: Leadership involves guiding, motivating, and directing a team or organization towards a shared vision or goal. Effective leaders inspire and empower others to achieve success. Example: "His leadership skills have fostered a positive and productive work environment."

10 workplace vocabulary words with their meanings and examples:

1. Employee - (noun) a person who works for someone else or a company
   Example: John is an employee at the IT department.

2. Manager – (noun) a person responsible for overseeing a team or department
Example: Sarah is the project manager for our marketing team.

3. Deadline – (noun) the time or date by which something must be completed
Example: We have a tight deadline to meet for this project.

4. Collaboration – (noun) the action of working together with others to achieve a common goal
Example: Our team's collaboration led to the successful completion of the project.

5. Performance – (noun) the execution or accomplishment of work or tasks
Example: The employee's performance has been outstanding this quarter.

6. Feedback – (noun) information provided in response to a task or behavior
Example: I appreciated the constructive feedback I received on my presentation.

7. Overtime – (adverb) time worked beyond normal working hours
Example: The team had to work overtime to meet the project deadline.

8. Training – (noun) the action of teaching skills or knowledge for a specific job or task

Example: New employees undergo extensive training to become familiar with our processes.

9. Productivity - (noun) the rate at which work is completed efficiently
Example: Improving communication can help boost productivity in the workplace.

10. Promotion - (noun) the advancement to a higher rank or position in a job
Example: After years of hard work, Emily finally received a promotion to manager.

2. Professional Communication Phrases:

a) "Can we touch base?": This phrase is used to suggest a brief meeting or conversation to discuss progress, updates, or next steps. Example: "Can we touch base tomorrow to go over the project timeline?"

b) "Let's circle back on that": This phrase is used to imply the need to revisit a topic or discussion at a later time. Example: "I need to gather more information; let's circle back on that next week."

c) "Please advise": This phrase is used to request guidance, input, or advice from someone. Example: "I am not sure how to proceed with this; please advise on the next steps."

d) "I'll take that action item": This phrase is used to indicate that one will take responsibility for a particular task or action. Example: "I'll take that action item and provide you with an update by the end of the day."

e) "Let's run it up the flagpole": This phrase is used to suggest presenting an idea or proposal for consideration or feedback. Example: "Let's run it up the flagpole and see what the team thinks."

50 Professional Communication Phrases with examples :

1. "Thank you for your attention to this matter."
    - Use: To express appreciation for someone's consideration or effort.
    - Example: "Thank you for your attention to this matter. Your feedback is highly valuable to us."

2. "As per our discussion earlier"
    - Use: Referring back to a previous conversation or meeting.
    - Example: "As per our discussion earlier, we will proceed with the plan as outlined."

3. "I appreciate your prompt response."
    - Use: Showing gratitude for a quick reply or action.
    - Example: "I appreciate your prompt response to my inquiry. It helps expedite the process."

4. "Please let me know if you need any further assistance."
    - Use: Offering help or support to someone.

- Example: "Please let me know if you need any further assistance with the project. I'm here to help."

5. "I would like to follow up on our earlier conversation."
 - Use: Politely reminding someone about a previous discussion.
 - Example: "I would like to follow up on our earlier conversation regarding the upcoming event logistics."

6. "Let's touch base next week to discuss the project's progress."
 - Use: Suggesting a future meeting or discussion.
 - Example: "Let's touch base next week to discuss the project's progress and address any challenges we may be facing."

7. "Could you please provide more details on this issue?"
 - Use: Requesting additional information or clarification.
 - Example: "Could you please provide more details on this issue so we can better understand the situation?"

8. "I apologize for any inconvenience this may have caused."
 - Use: Expressing regret for any trouble or inconvenience.
 - Example: "I apologize for any inconvenience this may have caused. We are working to resolve the issue promptly."

9. "I will look into this matter and get back to you shortly."
 - Use: Assuring someone you will investigate and provide an update.
 - Example: "I will look into this matter and get back to you shortly with more information on the issue."

10. "Your input is highly appreciated in helping us make better decisions."
   - Use: Acknowledging someone's contribution and feedback.
   - Example: "Your input is highly appreciated in helping us make better decisions. Thank you for sharing your insights."

11. "Let's schedule a meeting to discuss the upcoming project timeline."
   - Use: Proposing a meeting to focus on a specific topic.
   - Example: "Let's schedule a meeting to discuss the upcoming project timeline and allocate tasks accordingly."

12. "I understand your concerns and will address them accordingly."
   - Use: Acknowledging someone's worries and committing to resolve them.
   - Example: "I understand your concerns and will address them accordingly to ensure a smooth project execution."

13. "It would be great if we could collaborate on this to achieve our goals."
   - Use: Suggesting teamwork to reach shared objectives.
   - Example: "It would be great if we could collaborate on this to achieve our goals efficiently and effectively."

14. "If possible, please prepare a summary of your findings for the upcoming presentation."
   - Use: Requesting someone to compile information for a specific purpose.
   - Example: "If possible, please prepare a summary of your findings for the upcoming presentation to share with the team."

15. "With your expertise in this area, I believe we can overcome any challenges."
   - Use: Recognizing someone's skills and offering encouragement.
   - Example: "With your expertise in this area, I believe we can overcome any challenges that may come our way."

16. "I would like to acknowledge the hard work and dedication of the team on this project."
   - Use: Recognizing and appreciating the team's efforts.
   - Example: "I would like to acknowledge the hard work and dedication of the team on this project. Your commitment is truly commendable."

17. "Looking forward to your insights during the upcoming brainstorming session."
   - Use: Expressing anticipation for someone's contributions or ideas.
   - Example: "Looking forward to your insights during the upcoming brainstorming session. Your input will be valuable to the discussion."

18. "I will make sure to loop you in on any updates regarding this issue."
   - Use: Promising to keep someone informed about developments.
   - Example: "I will make sure to loop you in on any updates regarding this issue to ensure transparency and clear communication."

19. "Let's work together to find a solution that meets everyone's

needs."

- Use: Encouraging collaboration to reach a mutually beneficial solution.

- Example: "Let's work together to find a solution that meets everyone's needs and resolves the issue effectively."

20. "Could you clarify your expectations in more detail so we can align our approach?"

- Use: Seeking clarity on expectations to ensure mutual understanding.

- Example: "Could you clarify your expectations in more detail so we can align our approach and meet the desired outcomes?"

21. "Your dedication to quality work is evident in the results we have achieved."

- Use: Complimenting someone on their commitment to excellence.

- Example: "Your dedication to quality work is evident in the results we have achieved together. Keep up the great work!"

22. "In order to streamline the process, let's establish clear guidelines for the team."

- Use: Proposing a method to improve efficiency and clarity.

- Example: "In order to streamline the process, let's establish clear guidelines for the team to follow. This will help avoid confusion and promote consistency."

23. "I appreciate your flexibility in adjusting to the new timeline."

- Use: Acknowledging someone's adaptability and openness

to change.

- Example: "I appreciate your flexibility in adjusting to the new timeline. Your willingness to adapt is crucial for the success of the project."

24. "Please let me know if there are any constraints we need to consider for this task."

- Use: Requesting information on limitations or restrictions.
- Example: "Please let me know if there are any constraints we need to consider for this task, so we can plan accordingly and avoid any challenges."

25. "I am confident that with our combined efforts, we can achieve our goals."

- Use: Expressing belief in teamwork and collective success.
- Example: "I am confident that with our combined efforts, we can achieve our goals and deliver exceptional results."

26. "Your attention to detail has contributed significantly to the success of this project."

- Use: Recognizing someone's meticulousness and its impact on outcomes.
- Example: "Your attention to detail has contributed significantly to the success of this project. Your thoroughness is truly commendable."

27. "Let's explore different strategies to enhance our marketing campaign."

- Use: Proposing a collaborative approach to improve a specific area.
- Example: "Let's explore different strategies to enhance

our marketing campaign and reach our target audience more effectively."

28. "I value your feedback and will take it into consideration for future improvements."
   - Use: Showing appreciation for input and commitment to use it constructively.
   - Example: "I value your feedback and will take it into consideration for future improvements to ensure we meet our objectives."

29. "Could we set up a meeting to discuss the project milestones and deadlines?"
   - Use: Proposing a meeting to review project progress and timelines.
   - Example: "Could we set up a meeting to discuss the project milestones and deadlines to ensure we are on track with our deliverables?"

30. "Your leadership in this role has inspired the team to perform at their best."
   - Use: Acknowledging someone's impact as a leader and motivator.
   - Example: "Your leadership in this role has inspired the team to perform at their best and strive for excellence. Your guidance is truly invaluable."

31. "To optimize our workflow, let's identify areas for process improvement."
   - Use: Suggesting a strategy to enhance efficiency and productivity.

- Example: "To optimize our workflow, let's identify areas for process improvement and implement changes that will streamline our operations."

32. "I see great potential in your ideas and look forward to seeing them implemented."
 - Use: Recognizing creative thinking and expressing enthusiasm for its implementation.
 - Example: "I see great potential in your ideas and look forward to seeing them implemented to enhance our strategies and drive innovation."

33. "Let's establish regular check-ins to monitor progress and address any challenges."
 - Use: Proposing a method to stay updated on developments and address obstacles.
 - Example: "Let's establish regular check-ins to monitor progress and address any challenges that may arise, ensuring we stay on track with our goals."

34. "I trust your judgment in making decisions that align with our company's values."
 - Use: Expressing confidence in someone's decision-making abilities.
 - Example: "I trust your judgment in making decisions that align with our company's values and contribute to our overall mission."

35. "Can you provide an update on the status of the project deliverables?"
 - Use: Requesting information on the current progress of

project tasks.
- Example: "Can you provide an update on the status of the project deliverables so we can assess our timeline and resources accordingly?"

36. "Your creativity has added a unique perspective to our marketing strategies."
- Use: Appreciating someone's innovation and its impact on approaches.
- Example: "Your creativity has added a unique perspective to our marketing strategies, making our campaigns more engaging and effective."

37. "Let's brainstorm ideas together to find the best solution for this challenge."
- Use: Suggesting collaborative problem-solving to overcome obstacles.
- Example: "Let's brainstorm ideas together to find the best solution for this challenge and ensure we address it comprehensively."

38. "I appreciate your transparency in communication, as it fosters trust within the team."
- Use: Acknowledging honest and open communication and its positive effects.
- Example: "I appreciate your transparency in communication, as it fosters trust within the team and promotes a supportive work environment."

39. "Please provide your insights on how we can improve our customer service process."

- Use: Requesting feedback and suggestions for enhancing a specific aspect.
   - Example: "Please provide your insights on how we can improve our customer service process to better meet our clients' needs and expectations."

40. "Your commitment to excellence sets a high standard for the team to aspire to."
   - Use: Recognizing someone's dedication to quality and its influence on others.
   - Example: "Your commitment to excellence sets a high standard for the team to aspire to, motivating us to deliver our best work."

41. "Let's set up a training session to enhance our skills in this area."
   - Use: Suggesting a training opportunity to improve competencies.
   - Example: "Let's set up a training session to enhance our skills in this area and stay updated on the latest trends and practices."

42. "I believe your expertise can greatly contribute to the success of this project."
   - Use: Recognizing someone's knowledge and its potential impact.
   - Example: "I believe your expertise can greatly contribute to the success of this project by providing valuable insights and guidance."

43. "In recognition of your hard work, we would like to

commend you for your achievements."

- Use: Acknowledging and celebrating someone's accomplishments.

- Example: "In recognition of your hard work, we would like to commend you for your achievements and dedication to excellence."

44. "I value your opinion and would like to hear your thoughts on this matter."

- Use: Showing respect for someone's viewpoint and inviting their input.

- Example: "I value your opinion and would like to hear your thoughts on this matter to gain a better understanding of various perspectives."

45. "Let's allocate resources wisely to ensure efficient project management."

- Use: Emphasizing the importance of resource allocation for effective operations.

- Example: "Let's allocate resources wisely to ensure efficient project management and optimize our outcomes within the designated timeframe."

46. "Your professionalism in handling challenging situations is truly commendable."

- Use: Acknowledging someone's composure and professionalism under pressure.

- Example: "Your professionalism in handling challenging situations is truly commendable and reflects well on the entire team."

47. "I appreciate your proactive approach in addressing potential issues before they escalate."
   - Use: Recognizing someone's initiative in problem-solving and prevention.
   - Example: "I appreciate your proactive approach in addressing potential issues before they escalate, showing foresight and strategic thinking."

48. "Could we set up a debriefing session to review the outcomes of the project?"
   - Use: Suggesting a meeting to analyze results and lessons learned.
   - Example: "Could we set up a debriefing session to review the outcomes of the project and identify areas for improvement in our future endeavors?"

49. "Your contribution to the team has been invaluable, and we are grateful for your efforts."
   - Use: Expressing gratitude for someone's significant role and impact.
   - Example: "Your contribution to the team has been invaluable, and we are grateful for your efforts in achieving our goals together."

50. "Let's collaborate to develop a strategic plan that aligns with our long-term objectives."
   - Use: Proposing teamwork to create a plan in line with organizational goals.
   - Example: "Let's collaborate to develop a strategic plan that aligns with our long-term objectives and ensures sustainable growth for the organization."

3. Industry-Specific Vocabulary:

a) Tech Industry:

i) Agile Methodology: Agile methodology is an iterative approach to software development that emphasizes flexibility, collaboration, and continuous improvement. Example: "Our team follows Agile methodology to adapt to changing requirements and deliver high-quality products."

ii) SaaS (Software as a Service): SaaS is a software distribution model where applications are hosted by a third-party provider and made available to customers over the internet. Example: "Our company offers SaaS solutions for seamless data management."

b) Finance Industry:

i) ROI (Return on Investment): ROI is a financial metric used to evaluate the profitability of an investment relative to its cost. Example: "We need to analyze the ROI of this marketing campaign to determine its success."

ii) Hedge Fund: A hedge fund is an investment fund that pools capital from accredited individuals or institutional investors and employs various strategies to maximize returns. Example: "He manages a hedge fund that specializes in global macroeconomic trends."

c) Healthcare Industry:

i) EHR (Electronic Health Record): EHR is a digital version of a patient's paper chart that contains medical history, diagnoses, medications, treatment plans, and more. Example: "The hospital implemented an EHR system to improve patient care coordination."

ii) PPO (Preferred Provider Organization): PPO is a type of health insurance plan that offers a network of healthcare providers for covered services at a discounted rate. Example: "Our insurance plan includes access to a wide network of providers through a PPO."

4. Work Ethic and Soft Skills Terminology:

a) Proactive: Being proactive involves taking initiative, anticipating needs, and actively seeking solutions without waiting to be told what to do. Example: "His proactive approach to problem-solving saved the team time and effort."

b) Adaptability: Adaptability is the ability to adjust to new situations, challenges, or changes in the workplace. It is a valuable skill that enables individuals to thrive in dynamic environments. Example: "She demonstrated remarkable adaptability during the company restructuring."

c) Resilience: Resilience is the capacity to bounce back from setbacks, adversity, or failures. Resilient individuals can maintain a positive attitude and continue striving towards their goals. Example: "Despite facing challenges, her resilience shone through, and she emerged stronger."

d) Emotional Intelligence: Emotional intelligence refers to the ability to recognize, understand, and manage one's emotions and effectively navigate social interactions. Example: "His high emotional intelligence enables him to build strong relationships with colleagues and clients."

e) Time Management: Time management involves planning, organizing, and prioritizing tasks to make efficient use of time and meet deadlines. Effective time management is crucial for productivity and success in the workplace. Example: "Improving time management skills helped her complete projects ahead of schedule."

50 industry-specific vocabulary terms along with examples:

1. SEO (Search Engine Optimization): Improving website visibility in search engine results. Example: "We need to focus on SEO to boost our website traffic."

2. ROI (Return on Investment): Measure of the profitability of an investment. Example: "We saw a high ROI from our latest marketing campaign."

3. KPIs (Key Performance Indicators): Quantifiable metrics used to evaluate the success of an organization or project. Example: "Our KPIs include conversion rate and customer retention."

4. B2B (Business-to-Business): Transactions between businesses. Example: "Our company specializes in B2B software solutions."

5. B2C (Business-to-Consumer): Transactions between businesses and consumers. Example: "We have a strong B2C marketing strategy for our new product launch."

6. CPC (Cost Per Click): The cost an advertiser pays for each click on their online ad. Example: "We are tracking CPC to maximize our advertising budget."

7. CRM (Customer Relationship Management): Strategies and technologies used to manage interactions with customers. Example: "Our CRM system helps us track customer inquiries and purchases."

8. SaaS (Software as a Service): Software delivery model where software is licensed on a subscription basis. Example: "We use SaaS solutions for our project management needs."

9. Lead Generation: The process of identifying and attracting potential customers. Example: "Our lead generation efforts have resulted in a 20% increase in sales."

10. Churn Rate: The rate at which customers stop doing business with a company. Example: "We need to reduce our churn rate by improving customer satisfaction."

11. Supply Chain: The sequence of processes involved in the production and distribution of a product. Example: "Our supply chain is optimized for efficiency and cost-effectiveness."

12. Freemium: A business model that offers basic services for free while charging for premium features. Example: "Our app

operates on a freemium model to attract users."

13. Omnichannel: Integrating multiple channels for a seamless customer experience. Example: "Our omnichannel strategy includes online, in-store, and mobile sales."

14. Influencer Marketing: Leveraging individuals with large followings to promote products or services. Example: "We partnered with influencers for our latest social media campaign."

15. Blockchain: A decentralized digital ledger technology used for secure transactions. Example: "Blockchain technology ensures transparency and security in our transactions."

16. LTV (Lifetime Value): The amount of revenue a customer is expected to generate over their lifetime. Example: "We calculate LTV to assess customer profitability."

17. SWOT Analysis: Strategic planning tool to assess Strengths, Weaknesses, Opportunities, and Threats. Example: "We conducted a SWOT analysis to evaluate our market position."

18. MVP (Minimum Viable Product): The most basic version of a product released to gather feedback. Example: "We launched our MVP to test market demand."

19. Agile: A project management methodology emphasizing flexibility and collaboration. Example: "Our team follows agile principles to adapt to changing requirements."

20. Brick-and-Mortar: Traditional physical stores as opposed

to online businesses. Example: "Our company has both brick-and-mortar locations and an online store."

21. ROAS (Return on Ad Spend): A marketing metric that measures the revenue generated from advertising relative to the cost of the advertising. Example: "Our ROAS for the last campaign was 5, meaning we earned $5 for every dollar spent on advertising."

22. API (Application Programming Interface): A set of rules and protocols for building and interacting with software applications. Example: "We use third-party APIs to integrate additional features into our platform."

23. MRR (Monthly Recurring Revenue): The amount of predictable revenue a business expects each month from subscription-based services. Example: "Our MRR has been steadily increasing as we acquire more subscribers."

24. Churn Prediction: Using data analytics to forecast which customers are likely to stop using a service. Example: "Our churn prediction model helps us proactively retain customers at risk of leaving."

25. Branding: Establishing a distinctive identity for a product or service. Example: "Our branding resonates with our target audience, leading to high brand loyalty."

26. Outsourcing: Contracting out certain business functions to external entities. Example: "We outsource our customer support to a specialized service provider to reduce costs."

27. Landing Page: A web page designed specifically to convert visitors into leads or customers. Example: "Our landing page features a clear call-to-action to encourage sign-ups."

28. Scalability: The capability of a system to handle growth without compromising performance. Example: "Our cloud-based infrastructure offers scalability to accommodate increasing user demands."

29. Segmentation: Dividing a market into distinct groups based on characteristics like demographics or behavior. Example: "We use customer segmentation to tailor our marketing campaigns to specific audiences."

30. Net Promoter Score (NPS): A metric measuring customer loyalty by asking how likely customers are to recommend a product or service. Example: "Our NPS indicates strong customer satisfaction and loyalty."

31. Growth Hacking: Innovative marketing strategies focused on rapid growth. Example: "We employed growth hacking techniques to quickly expand our user base."

32. A/B Testing: Comparing two versions of a webpage or marketing campaign to determine which performs better. Example: "We conducted A/B testing to optimize our email subject lines for higher open rates."

33. Bounce Rate: The percentage of visitors who leave a website after viewing only one page. Example: "Our goal is to reduce the bounce rate by improving website content and user experience."

34. Subscription Model: Offering products or services on a recurring payment basis. Example: "Our subscription model provides customers with regular access to new features and content."

35. Market Segmentation: Dividing a market into subsets to better target specific consumer groups. Example: "Our market segmentation strategy ensures that we reach diverse customer segments effectively."

36. Brand Equity: The value of a brand's reputation, perception, and recognition in the market. Example: "Our brand equity has grown over the years due to consistent quality and customer satisfaction."

37. Big Data: Large volumes of data that are analyzed to reveal patterns and insights. Example: "Our company leverages big data analytics to improve decision-making and understand consumer behavior."

38. Cross-Selling: Encouraging customers to purchase related or complementary products. Example: "We implemented a cross-selling strategy to increase the average order value."

39. Microtargeting: Tailoring marketing efforts to reach specific individuals or small audience segments. Example: "Our microtargeting campaign resulted in higher engagement and conversions."

40. Loyalty Program: Incentive program designed to retain customers and encourage repeat purchases. Example: "Our

loyalty program offers exclusive discounts and rewards to long-term customers."

41. Value Proposition: A promise of value that a product or service brings to customers. Example: "Our value proposition focuses on quality, affordability, and customer service."

42. Customer Acquisition Cost (CAC): The cost associated with acquiring a new customer. Example: "We aim to reduce our CAC by optimizing our marketing channels for better efficiency."

43. Market Share: The percentage of total sales within a market that a company captures. Example: "Our goal is to increase our market share by launching new products and entering new territories."

44. Virality: The rate at which a piece of content or product spreads through social sharing. Example: "The viral nature of our campaign led to a significant increase in brand awareness."

45. Competitive Analysis: Evaluating the strengths and weaknesses of competitors in a market. Example: "Our competitive analysis identified key areas where we can differentiate and gain a competitive edge."

46. E-commerce: Buying and selling goods or services online. Example: "Our e-commerce platform has seen a surge in sales due to changing consumer shopping habits."

47. Retargeting: Showing ads to users who have previously engaged with a website or product. Example: "We use retargeting

campaigns to bring back visitors who showed interest but did not make a purchase."

48. Upselling: Encouraging customers to buy a more expensive or upgraded version of a product. Example: "Our sales team is trained to upsell additional features to enhance customer value."

49. User Experience (UX): The overall experience a person has when interacting with a website or product. Example: "Our UX design focuses on simplicity and intuitive navigation for an optimal user experience."

50. SWOT Analysis: A strategic planning tool used to identify a company's Strengths, Weaknesses, Opportunities, and Threats. Example: "Conducting a SWOT analysis helped us understand our position in the market and develop effective strategies for growth."

5. Workplace Documentation and Reporting Terms:

a) KPIs (Key Performance Indicators): KPIs are quantifiable metrics used to evaluate the performance of an individual, team, department, or organization against strategic goals. Example: "Tracking KPIs helps us measure progress and identify areas for improvement."

b) SWOT Analysis: SWOT analysis is a strategic planning tool that assesses a business's Strengths, Weaknesses, Opportunities, and Threats to inform decision-making. Example: "Conducting a SWOT analysis revealed our competitive advantages and potential risks."

c) Quarterly Report: A quarterly report is a document that summarizes the organization's performance, achievements, challenges, and financial results over a three-month period. Example: "She is responsible for compiling the quarterly report to update stakeholders on our progress."

d) Executive Summary: An executive summary is a concise overview of a report, proposal, or presentation that highlights key points, findings, and recommendations. Example: "The executive summary provided a comprehensive overview of the market analysis."

e) Performance Review: A performance review is a formal assessment of an employee's work performance, strengths, areas for improvement, and goal-setting for future development. Example: "He had a positive performance review with constructive feedback for professional growth."

6. Workplace Etiquette and Professionalism:

a) Punctuality: Punctuality is the practice of arriving on time for meetings, appointments, and work obligations. It demonstrates respect for others' time and reliability. Example: "She is known for her punctuality and always arrives early for team meetings."

b) Respectful Communication: Respectful communication involves using polite language, active listening, and acknowledging different viewpoints to foster positive interactions with colleagues. Example: "Maintaining respectful communication is key to building strong relationships in the workplace."

c) Professional Attire: Professional attire refers to clothing that is appropriate for the workplace, reflecting the company's dress code and industry standards. Example: "Employees are expected to dress in professional attire for client meetings and presentations."

d) Conflict Resolution: Conflict resolution is the process of addressing and resolving disagreements, disputes, or conflicts constructively to maintain positive relationships and productivity. Example: "They engaged in open dialogue and effective conflict resolution to reach a mutually acceptable solution."

e) Networking: Networking involves establishing and nurturing relationships with professionals in similar or complementary fields to exchange information, opportunities, and support. Example: "Attending industry conferences is a great way to network and expand your professional contacts."

In conclusion, mastering common workplace vocabulary and phrases is vital for effective communication, collaboration, and professional growth. By understanding and utilizing these terms in various contexts, you can enhance your workplace interactions, build stronger relationships, and contribute to a positive and productive work environment. Whether you are engaging in general workplace discussions, industry-specific conversations, or soft skills development, having a solid grasp of relevant vocabulary and phrases will enable you to communicate with clarity, confidence, and professionalism.

4

Tips for Building Confidence in Speaking English at Work

Building confidence in speaking English at work is a crucial skill that can open up opportunities for professional growth and success. Whether you are a non-native English speaker or just looking to improve your communication skills, developing confidence in using English in the workplace can have a significant impact on your career. In this comprehensive guide, we will explore various strategies and tips for building confidence in speaking English at work, along with practical examples to illustrate each point.

1. Understand Your Audience: One of the first steps to building confidence in speaking English at work is understanding your audience. Consider who you are speaking to, their level of English proficiency, and their expectations. Tailoring your communication style to suit your audience can help you feel more confident and make your message more effective.

Example: If you are addressing a group of colleagues who are non-native English speakers, you may want to speak slowly and clearly, avoiding complex vocabulary or idiomatic expressions that could be difficult for them to understand.

2. Practice Active Listening: Active listening is a critical skill for effective communication in any language. By listening attentively to others, you can better understand their perspectives and respond appropriately. This can help build your confidence in engaging in English conversations at work.

Example: During team meetings, practice active listening by focusing on what others are saying, asking clarifying questions, and summarizing key points to demonstrate your understanding.

3. Build Vocabulary: Expanding your English vocabulary can boost your confidence in expressing yourself more precisely and confidently at work. Learn new words and phrases related to your industry or job role to enhance your communication skills.

Example: Create flashcards of new English words and review them regularly to reinforce your vocabulary. Use online resources like vocabulary-building apps or websites to expand your word bank.

4. Practice Speaking Regularly: Like any skill, speaking English confidently takes practice. Look for opportunities to practice speaking English at work, such as participating in meetings, presentations, or informal discussions with colleagues.

Example: Volunteer to present in team meetings or join English-speaking clubs or conversation groups to practice speaking regularly and receive feedback from others.

5. Set Realistic Goals: Setting achievable goals for improving your English speaking skills can help you stay motivated and focused. Break down your goals into smaller, manageable steps and track your progress over time.

Example: Set a goal to speak up at least once during each team meeting or aim to have a short conversation in English with a colleague every day to gradually build your confidence.

6. Seek Feedback: Feedback from others can provide valuable insights into your English speaking skills and areas for improvement. Ask for feedback from colleagues, supervisors, or language coaches to help you identify areas where you can enhance your communication.

Example: After a presentation or meeting where you spoke in English, ask a trusted colleague for feedback on your language use, pronunciation, or clarity of communication.

7. Embrace Mistakes: Making mistakes is a natural part of the learning process, especially when learning a new language. Instead of being afraid of making mistakes, embrace them as opportunities for growth and learning.

Example: If you mispronounce a word or use incorrect grammar in a conversation, acknowledge the mistake, correct yourself, and learn from it for future conversations.

8. Immerse Yourself in English: Surrounding yourself with English language content can help you immerse yourself in the language and become more comfortable with using it in various contexts. Watch English movies, read English books or articles, and listen to English podcasts to expose yourself to different styles of communication.

Example: Set aside time each day to engage with English language content, whether it's reading an article related to your industry, watching a TED talk in English, or listening to a podcast on leadership skills.

9. Role-play Scenarios: Practicing real-life scenarios through role-play can help you simulate English conversations you may encounter at work. Role-playing can give you the opportunity to practice specific language skills and gain confidence in using English in different situations.

Example: Pair up with a colleague and role-play a customer service scenario where you need to address a customer query or concern in English, practicing both your language skills and customer communication.

10. Use Positive Affirmations: Positive affirmations can help boost your confidence and mindset when speaking English at work. Remind yourself of your strengths, progress, and capabilities in using English, fostering a positive attitude towards language learning.

Example: Before a challenging English presentation, repeat positive affirmations such as "I am improving my English skills every day" or "I am confident in expressing myself in English" to build a positive mindset.

11. Record Yourself: Recording yourself speaking in English can provide valuable insights into your communication skills, including pronunciation, intonation, and clarity. Listen to the recordings to identify areas for improvement and track your progress over time.

Example: Use a voice recording app on your phone to record yourself practicing English conversations, presentations, or speeches. Listen to the recordings to evaluate your speaking skills and make adjustments as needed.

12. Stay Calm and Relaxed: Feeling nervous or anxious when speaking English at work can hinder your confidence. Practice mindfulness techniques, deep breathing exercises, or visualization to stay calm and relaxed before and during English conversations or presentations.

Example: Before a job interview conducted in English, take a few minutes to practice deep breathing exercises to calm your nerves and focus your thoughts on communicating effectively.

13. Celebrate Your Progress: Recognize and celebrate your achievements and progress in building confidence in speaking English at work. Acknowledge the small wins along the way, whether it's successfully leading a meeting in English or having a fluent conversation with a client.

Example: Keep a journal of your language learning journey and write down your accomplishments, no matter how small they may seem. Treat yourself to a small reward or celebration for each milestone you reach.

14. Use Visual Aids: Visual aids can enhance your communication and help you convey your message more effectively in English. Use slides, diagrams, charts, and other visual tools to support your verbal communication and increase audience engagement.

Example: When presenting a project update in English, create visual slides with key data points, timelines, and graphics to supplement your spoken presentation and help your audience better understand the information.

15. Engage in Small Talk: Engaging in small talk with colleagues in English can help you practice casual conversations, build relationships, and feel more comfortable using English in informal settings at work.

Example: Initiate a conversation with a coworker in the break room or during a coffee break by asking about their weekend plans, sharing a funny anecdote, or discussing a common interest in English.

16. Practice Pronunciation: Improving your pronunciation in English can enhance your overall clarity and confidence when speaking at work. Work on pronouncing individual sounds, words, and phrases correctly to be better understood by others.

Example: Practice tongue twisters or phonetic exercises to

improve your pronunciation of challenging English sounds or words. Record yourself practicing pronunciation and compare it to native speakers for accuracy.

17. Engage in Language Exchange: Participating in language exchange programs or finding a language partner can offer you the chance to practice speaking English with native speakers or other learners. Language exchanges can help you improve your conversational fluency and cultural understanding.

Example: Join an online language exchange platform or a local meetup group to connect with native English speakers interested in learning your native language. Practice speaking English with them in exchange for practicing their language.

18. Seek Professional Development: Investing in professional development opportunities related to language learning or communication skills can help you build confidence in speaking English at work. Attend language workshops, enroll in English courses, or work with a language coach to enhance your skills.

Example: Sign up for a business English course that focuses on improving communication in professional settings, such as business meetings, negotiations, and presentations, to sharpen your language skills for the workplace.

19. Visualize Success: Visualizing yourself speaking confidently in English at work can help you mentally prepare for challenging situations and build a positive mindset. Imagine yourself delivering a successful presentation, leading a productive meeting, or engaging in a fluent conversation in English.

Example: Before a job interview conducted in English, visualize yourself answering questions confidently, maintaining eye contact, and articulating your thoughts clearly to create a positive mental image of success.

20. Learn from Role Models: Identify successful communicators or English speakers in your field and learn from their communication style, language use, and strategies for building confidence. Observing and emulating role models can inspire you to improve your own English speaking skills.

Example: Watch TED talks or presentations by influential speakers in your industry to study their speaking techniques, language choices, and persuasive communication strategies that you can incorporate into your own English speaking practice.

21. Maintain a Growth Mindset: Adopting a growth mindset towards language learning can help you stay motivated, resilient, and open to feedback and challenges. Embrace the process of learning English as a continuous journey of improvement and development.

Example: When faced with a language barrier or a difficult communication task, view it as an opportunity to learn and grow rather than as a roadblock. Approach challenges with a positive attitude and a willingness to learn from your experiences.

22. Practice Intonation and Stress: Pay attention to intonation patterns and word stress in English to convey meaning and emotion effectively in your spoken communication. Practice

varying your intonation and emphasizing key words to enhance your expressiveness in English.

Example: Practice reading aloud English sentences with different intonation patterns, emphasizing specific words to convey different emotions or emphasis. Listen to English speakers or watch English movies to study natural intonation and stress patterns.

23. Use Language Learning Apps: Leveraging language learning apps and online platforms can provide you with interactive exercises, quizzes, and resources to improve your English speaking skills. Choose apps that focus on conversation practice, pronunciation, vocabulary building, and listening comprehension.

Example: Download language learning apps like Duolingo, Babbel, HelloTalk, or FluentU to supplement your English language learning and practice speaking skills through interactive exercises, games, and conversation practice.

24. Diversify Your Reading Material: Reading a variety of English texts, such as articles, reports, business emails, or industry publications, can expose you to different writing styles, vocabulary, and expressions. Diversifying your reading material can broaden your language skills and help you communicate more effectively in English.

Example: Subscribe to online newsletters, blogs, or publications related to your field of work and read articles or reports in English regularly to stay updated on industry trends, terminology, and communication styles.

25. Network with English Speakers: Building connections with English speakers in your professional network can offer you opportunities to practice speaking English, seek advice or feedback, and learn from their experiences. Networking can help you expand your language skills and build confidence in using English in a professional context.

Example: Attend networking events, conferences, or industry seminars where you can interact with English-speaking professionals, exchange ideas, and engage in conversations to improve your English communication skills and expand your network.

26. Join Toastmasters or Public Speaking Groups: Joining Toastmasters International or local public speaking groups can provide you with a supportive environment to practice speaking English, receive constructive feedback, and improve your public speaking skills. Participating in public speaking sessions can boost your confidence and communication abilities in English.

Example: Participate in Toastmasters club meetings or public speaking workshops where you can give speeches in English, receive evaluations from peers, and practice impromptu speaking to enhance your English language fluency and confidence.

27. Use Language Resources: Taking advantage of online language resources, such as grammar guides, pronunciation tutorials, language learning websites, and online courses, can supplement your English language learning and provide you with additional support in mastering the language.

Example: Explore language resources like Grammarly, BBC Learning English, Purdue OWL, or Cambridge English online tools to access grammar explanations, pronunciation guides, interactive exercises, and language quizzes to enhance your English skills.

28. Create a Language Learning Plan: Developing a structured language learning plan with clear goals, milestones, and learning strategies can help you stay organized, focused, and consistent in improving your English speaking skills. Create a personalized plan that aligns with your learning objectives and schedule.

Example: Create a weekly language learning schedule that includes activities like vocabulary practice, listening exercises, speaking drills, and reading assignments to ensure a well-rounded approach to improving your English communication skills over time.

29. Apply Language Skills in Real-Life Situations: Applying your English language skills in real-life situations, such as ordering in English at a restaurant, making phone calls in English, or attending networking events, can help you practice using the language authentically and build confidence in your ability to communicate effectively in English.

Example: Challenge yourself to engage in English conversations outside of work, such as ordering food in English at a local restaurant or striking up conversations with English speakers at social events, to practice your language skills in real-world settings.

30. Stay Consistent and Persistent: Consistency and persistence are key to improving your English speaking skills and building confidence over time. Make a commitment to practice regularly, set aside dedicated time for language learning, and stay motivated to progress in your language proficiency.

Example: Set aside a specific time each day for English language practice, whether it's early in the morning, during lunch breaks, or in the evening, to stay consistent in building your language skills and developing confidence in speaking English at work.

In conclusion, building confidence in speaking English at work requires a combination of practice, dedication, and a positive mindset. By implementing the tips and strategies outlined in this guide, you can enhance your English communication skills, overcome language barriers, and feel more confident in using English in professional settings. Remember that building confidence is a gradual process that requires patience, perseverance, and a willingness to step out of your comfort zone. With consistent effort and a proactive approach to language learning, you can improve your English speaking skills, boost your confidence, and advance your career opportunities in the global workplace.

100 Tips for Building Confidence in Speaking English at Work

1. Set small goals for yourself to practice speaking English daily.
2. Have confidence in your abilities and ignore self-doubt.
3. Focus on your strengths and how far you've come in learning English.

4. Practice speaking with a friend or colleague who can offer constructive feedback.

5. Engage in English conversation groups or clubs to improve your skills.

6. Use language learning apps to practice speaking and get instant feedback.

7. Listen to podcasts or watch English TV shows to improve your pronunciation and fluency.

8. Record yourself speaking and listen back to identify areas for improvement.

9. Celebrate small victories in your language learning journey.

10. Take breaks when you feel overwhelmed and come back to practicing with a fresh perspective.

11. Remember that making mistakes is a natural part of learning a new language.

12. Embrace opportunities to speak English, even if you feel nervous.

13. Use positive affirmations to boost your confidence before speaking in English.

14. Surround yourself with supportive people who encourage your language learning efforts.

15. Keep a journal of your progress in speaking English to track your improvement over time.

16. Visualize successful conversations in English to build confidence in your abilities.

17. Practice deep breathing exercises to calm your nerves before speaking.

18. Engage in role-playing scenarios to practice speaking in different contexts.

19. Learn and use common English phrases used in the workplace to feel more comfortable.

20. Set aside dedicated time each day to focus on improving your English speaking skills.

21. Seek feedback from native English speakers to help refine your pronunciation.

22. Stay consistent in your language learning efforts to see steady progress.

23. Challenge yourself with more complex language tasks as your confidence grows.

24. Reward yourself for reaching language learning milestones.

25. Join online language exchange platforms to practice speaking English with others.

26. Find a language learning buddy to practice speaking English together.

27. Watch TED Talks or presentations in English to observe effective communication techniques.

28. Record yourself giving presentations or speeches in English to build confidence.

29. Attend English language workshops or seminars to improve your speaking skills.

30. Immerse yourself in English-speaking environments to practice speaking naturally.

31. Practice mirroring the intonation and rhythm of native English speakers.

32. Engage in debates or discussions in English to strengthen your communication skills.

33. Set realistic goals for your language learning journey to avoid feeling overwhelmed.

34. Use flashcards to learn new vocabulary and improve your speaking skills.

35. Engage in language games or challenges to make practic-

ing English fun.

36. Visualize yourself as a confident English speaker to boost your self-assurance.

37. Take note of your progress and celebrate improvements in your speaking abilities.

38. Participate in language challenges or contests to push yourself out of your comfort zone.

39. Be patient with yourself and remember that progress takes time.

40. Practice speaking English in front of a mirror to work on your nonverbal communication.

41. Listen to English music and try to sing along to improve your pronunciation.

42. Engage in language exchange programs to practice speaking with native English speakers.

43. Work on your accent by listening to how native speakers pronounce words.

44. Join public speaking clubs or workshops to gain confidence in speaking English.

45. Remind yourself of your past successes in learning English to boost your confidence.

46. Learn about cultural nuances and idioms to improve your understanding of English conversations.

47. Engage in mock interviews in English to prepare for professional interactions.

48. Use language learning websites and apps to practice speaking exercises.

49. Attend language meetups or networking events to practice speaking English.

50. Practice active listening during conversations to improve your speaking skills.

51. Seek out opportunities to give presentations or workshops in English.

52. Practice speaking about topics you're passionate about to boost your confidence.

53. Engage in language immersion experiences to practice speaking English in real-life situations.

54. Use visual aids or props to help illustrate your points during English conversations.

55. Ask for feedback from peers or mentors to help pinpoint areas for improvement.

56. Practice speaking in front of a camera to get used to being recorded.

57. Join online speaking clubs or forums to practice speaking English with others.

58. Take language proficiency tests to evaluate your progress and set new goals.

59. Use language learning resources tailored to workplace communication skills.

60. Practice speaking English in different professional settings to adapt your language skills.

61. Seek out opportunities to participate in group discussions or meetings in English.

62. Engage in language learning challenges on social media to stay motivated.

63. Create a language learning schedule to ensure consistent practice.

64. Practice speaking English with varying speeds to improve your fluency.

65. Use language learning apps with speech recognition technology to receive feedback on your pronunciation.

66. Engage in public speaking exercises to build confidence

in speaking to larger audiences.

67. Enroll in language courses focused on workplace communication skills.

68. Use language learning platforms to connect with native English speakers for practice.

69. Develop a vocabulary list of commonly used terms in your field to enhance your workplace communication.

70. Attend language workshops or seminars to learn strategies for effective communication in English.

71. Listen to English business podcasts or audiobooks to improve your professional vocabulary.

72. Record yourself giving elevator pitches or introductions in English to refine your communication skills.

73. Role-play professional scenarios in English to practice workplace communication.

74. Practice summarizing articles or reports in English to improve your speaking skills.

75. Participate in group projects or presentations in English to enhance collaboration skills.

76. Use business English resources to learn industry-specific terminology and expressions.

77. Engage in negotiations or debates in English to practice persuasion and argumentation skills.

78. Seek out opportunities to network with English-speaking professionals to practice your communication skills.

79. Attend English language conferences or webinars to immerse yourself in industry-specific topics.

80. Join online communities focused on professional English communication to connect with like-minded individuals.

81. Practice active listening during meetings or presentations to improve your comprehension and communication skills.

82. Engage in role-playing exercises to simulate workplace scenarios in English.

83. Create a portfolio of your English language achievements to track your progress and motivate yourself.

84. Use language learning software with interactive speaking exercises to practice workplace dialogues.

85. Attend seminars or workshops on public speaking in English to hone your presentation skills.

86. Collaborate on English writing projects to improve your written and oral communication.

87. Watch videos of professional English speakers to observe their language use and communication styles.

88. Seek feedback from colleagues or supervisors on your English communication skills to identify areas for improvement.

89. Use language learning resources that focus on business communication and etiquette.

90. Practice giving feedback or conducting performance reviews in English to enhance your professional communication skills.

91. Engage in cross-cultural communication exercises to understand different communication styles in English-speaking workplaces.

92. Create a personal brand statement in English to articulate your professional identity and goals.

93. Use English language resources to learn about industry trends and developments in your field.

94. Participate in English language book clubs or discussion groups to practice analytical thinking and communication skills.

95. Listen to English language TED Talks or webinars to stay informed about current topics and improve your listening skills.

96. Engage in English language debates or discussions with

colleagues to practice critical thinking and argumentation.

97. Attend virtual networking events or conferences in English to expand your professional network and practice your communication skills.

98. Participate in mock interviews or elevator pitch exercises in English to prepare for job opportunities.

99. Collaborate on English language projects or presentations with colleagues to enhance your teamwork and communication skills.

100. Reflect on your language learning journey and celebrate your achievements to boost your confidence in speaking English at work.

5

Navigating Cultural Differences in Communication

In today's interconnected world, effective communication is crucial for building relationships, conducting business, and fostering understanding among people from diverse cultural backgrounds. However, navigating cultural differences in communication can be a complex and challenging task. Cultural variations in norms, values, beliefs, and communication styles can lead to misunderstandings, misinterpretations, and conflicts if not managed carefully. In this essay, we will explore the importance of understanding cultural differences in communication, discuss key cultural dimensions that influence communication, and provide practical strategies and examples for navigating cultural diversities in various contexts.

Importance of Understanding Cultural Differences in Communication

Cultural differences play a significant role in shaping how

people communicate and interpret messages. When individuals from different cultural backgrounds interact, they bring their unique set of values, attitudes, behaviors, and communication styles to the conversation. Misunderstandings may arise if these differences are not recognized and accommodated. Therefore, understanding cultural variations in communication is essential for several reasons:

1. Effective Communication: Recognizing cultural differences helps individuals communicate more effectively by adjusting their communication style, language use, and nonverbal cues to suit the cultural preferences of their interlocutors.

2. Building Relationships: Acknowledging and respecting cultural diversities fosters trust, mutual respect, and empathy, which are essential for building strong interpersonal relationships across cultures.

3. Avoiding Misinterpretations: Awareness of cultural differences can prevent misunderstandings, misinterpretations, and unintended offense that may occur due to cultural insensitivity or ignorance.

4. Enhancing Collaboration: When individuals understand and respect cultural differences, they can collaborate more successfully, share diverse perspectives, and leverage each other's strengths to achieve common goals.

5. Cross-Cultural Competence: Developing cross-cultural competence through intercultural communication skills is becoming increasingly important in a globalized world where

people from different cultures interact regularly.

Cultural Dimensions Influencing Communication

To navigate cultural differences effectively, it is helpful to understand key cultural dimensions that shape communication styles and behaviors. Several frameworks have been developed to categorize and compare cultural values and behaviors across different societies. One of the most well-known frameworks is Geert Hofstede's cultural dimensions theory, which identifies six dimensions that influence cultural communication patterns:

1. Power Distance: Power distance refers to the extent to which less powerful members of a society accept and expect unequal distribution of power. In high power distance cultures, hierarchical structures and status differences are more pronounced, leading to indirect communication and deference to authority figures. In low power distance cultures, communication tends to be more egalitarian and direct.

Example: In a high power distance culture like Japan, subordinates may use formal language and indirect communication to show respect to their superiors. In contrast, in a low power distance culture like the United States, colleagues may address each other more informally and directly regardless of their hierarchical positions.

2. Individualism vs. Collectivism: Individualism reflects the degree to which individuals prioritize personal goals and autonomy over group interests, while collectivism emphasizes group harmony, collective well-being, and loyalty to the community.

In individualistic cultures, communication tends to be assertive, direct, and focused on individual achievements, whereas in collectivist cultures, communication is more group-oriented, harmonious, and relationship-driven.

Example: In individualistic cultures like the United States, communication may emphasize individual accomplishments, self-expression, and personal success. In collectivist cultures like China, communication may prioritize group cohesion, harmony, and the needs of the community.

3. Masculinity vs. Femininity: Masculinity refers to cultures that place a high value on competition, assertiveness, and material success, while femininity emphasizes cooperation, nurturing, and quality of life. Masculine cultures tend to value assertive communication styles, achievement orientation, and a focus on task accomplishment, whereas feminine cultures value collaboration, empathy, and relationship building.

Example: In masculine cultures like Japan, communication may be more competitive, goal-oriented, and focused on performance outcomes. In feminine cultures like Sweden, communication may be more inclusive, consensus-driven, and oriented toward nurturing relationships.

4. Uncertainty Avoidance: Uncertainty avoidance relates to the extent to which a culture tolerates ambiguity, uncertainty, and risk. Cultures high in uncertainty avoidance prefer clear rules, structured communication, and predictability to reduce uncertainty, while cultures low in uncertainty avoidance are more open to change, ambiguity, and innovative communica-

tion approaches.

Example: In high uncertainty avoidance cultures like Germany, communication may emphasize detailed planning, explicit instructions, and adherence to established norms to reduce uncertainty. In low uncertainty avoidance cultures like Denmark, communication may be more flexible, open to new ideas, and comfortable with ambiguity and risk.

5. Long-Term Orientation: Long-term orientation reflects the degree to which a culture values long-term goals, perseverance, and thrift over short-term gains and immediate gratification. Cultures high in long-term orientation prioritize persistence, endurance, and investment in the future, while cultures low in long-term orientation focus more on the present, tradition, and immediate results.

Example: In high long-term orientation cultures like China, communication may emphasize planning for the future, building relationships over time, and honoring traditions. In low long-term orientation cultures like the United States, communication may focus more on short-term goals, immediate results, and adapting to changing circumstances.

6. Indulgence vs. Restraint: The indulgence-restraint dimension refers to the extent to which a culture allows gratification of basic human desires and impulses. Cultures high in indulgence value individual happiness, leisure, and personal fulfillment, whereas cultures low in indulgence emphasize self-discipline, self-control, and restraint of impulses.

Example: In high indulgence cultures like Brazil, communication may include expressions of emotion, spontaneity, and enjoyment of life without strict social norms restricting behavior. In low indulgence cultures like Japan, communication may involve more self-discipline, modesty, and restraint in expressing emotions.

Practical Strategies for Navigating Cultural Differences in Communication

To navigate cultural differences effectively and foster positive intercultural communication, individuals can employ several strategies and tactics that promote understanding, respect, and effective collaboration across cultural boundaries. Some practical strategies for navigating cultural diversities in communication include:

1. Develop Cultural Awareness: Begin by educating yourself about the cultural norms, values, and communication styles of the people you are interacting with. Be curious, open-minded, and willing to learn about different cultural perspectives.

Example: Before traveling to Japan for a business meeting, take the time to research Japanese cultural practices, etiquette, and communication norms to avoid unintended misunderstandings or cultural faux pas.

2. Practice Active Listening: Cultivate active listening skills by paying attention to verbal cues, nonverbal gestures, tone of voice, and cultural nuances in communication. Avoid making assumptions or jumping to conclusions based on your own

cultural background.

Example: During a cross-cultural negotiation, practice active listening by paraphrasing, seeking clarification, and summarizing key points to demonstrate your understanding and respect for the other party's viewpoint.

3. Adapt Your Communication Style: Adjust your communication style, language use, tone, and nonverbal cues to align with the cultural preferences of your audience. Be flexible, empathetic, and sensitive to cultural differences in communication norms.

Example: When working with colleagues from diverse cultural backgrounds, adapt your communication style by using clear and direct language with some individuals while being more indirect and diplomatic with others based on their cultural expectations of communication.

4. Respect Cultural Norms: Show respect for the cultural norms, values, traditions, and customs of the people you are communicating with. Be mindful of taboos, sensitivities, and etiquette rules to demonstrate cultural competence and sensitivity.

Example: When attending a formal dinner in South Korea, observe and follow the protocol of using both hands to receive and offer gifts, removing shoes before entering homes, and showing deference to elders or authority figures.

5. Build Rapport and Trust: Focus on building rapport, trust, and

positive relationships with individuals from different cultural backgrounds by demonstrating empathy, warmth, and respect. Invest time in getting to know the person beyond surface-level interactions.

Example: Before discussing business matters with a potential partner from India, take the time to establish a personal connection, show genuine interest in their background, and engage in small talk to build trust and rapport.

6. Clarify Misunderstandings: Address misunderstandings, miscommunications, or conflicts promptly by seeking clarification, providing feedback, and resolving issues in a respectful and collaborative manner. Avoid blaming or attributing misunderstandings solely to cultural differences.

Example: If a miscommunication occurs during a virtual meeting with colleagues from different countries, acknowledge the misunderstanding, clarify the intended message, and seek feedback to ensure mutual understanding and avoid further confusion.

7. Use Language Appropriately: Be mindful of language barriers, language proficiency levels, and potential language misunderstandings in cross-cultural communication. Use simple language, avoid jargon or idiomatic expressions, and consider using translation or interpretation services when needed.

Example: When communicating with international clients who speak English as a second language, use clear and simple language, avoid slang or complex vocabulary, and provide written materials or visual aids to supplement verbal communication.

8. Embrace Diversity: Embrace cultural diversity, multiculturalism, and inclusive communication practices by valuing and celebrating the differences, perspectives, and contributions of individuals from varied cultural backgrounds. Create a supportive and inclusive environment that respects and appreciates cultural diversities.

Example: Organize cultural awareness training, diversity workshops, or cross-cultural events within your organization to promote understanding, empathy, and appreciation of different cultural backgrounds and perspectives among employees.

9. Seek Feedback and Learn: Be open to feedback, constructive criticism, and suggestions for improvement from individuals of different cultural backgrounds. Use feedback as an opportunity to learn, grow, and enhance your intercultural communication skills.

Example: After completing a cross-cultural project with a diverse team, solicit feedback from team members on the effectiveness of communication, areas for improvement, and lessons learned to enhance future cross-cultural collaborations.

10. Continuous Learning and Adaptation: Cultivate a growth mindset, curiosity, and willingness to learn from diverse cultural experiences, interactions, and feedback. Adapt and refine your communication skills based on ongoing reflection and self-awareness.

Example: Engage in cross-cultural exchanges, language immersion programs, cultural events, or international travel experiences to expand your cultural awareness, deepen your intercultural competence, and broaden your perspective on global communication.

Conclusion

Navigating cultural differences in communication is a multifaceted and dynamic process that requires awareness, sensitivity, adaptability, and open-mindedness. By understanding key cultural dimensions that influence communication styles, individuals can develop effective strategies for fostering cross-cultural understanding, collaboration, and positive relationships. Through practical examples and strategies for navigating cultural diversities in communication, individuals can enhance their intercultural communication skills, build cultural competence, and bridge the communication gap between people from diverse cultural backgrounds. By embracing cultural diversity, respecting cultural norms, and practicing empathy and inclusivity, individuals can create a more interconnected and harmonious global community based on mutual understanding, respect, and effective communication across cultural boundaries.

6

Polite and Professional Language in the Office

Professional communication in the workplace is essential for maintaining a positive and productive environment. Polite and professional language plays a significant role in ensuring effective communication among colleagues, superiors, and clients. In this essay, we will delve deeply into the importance of using polite and professional language in the office setting and provide examples to illustrate best practices.

1. Importance of Polite and Professional Language in the Office:

Effective communication is the cornerstone of any successful organization. Polite and professional language sets the tone for interactions in the workplace. It conveys respect, civility, and professionalism, fostering a positive work culture and enhancing productivity. Here are some key reasons why using polite and professional language is crucial in the office:

a. Establishing a Positive Work Environment:

Polite and professional language creates a positive work environment where employees feel respected and valued. It sets the standard for respectful interactions and promotes a culture of collaboration and mutual understanding. When colleagues communicate politely, it enhances teamwork and fosters a sense of camaraderie.

b. Building Strong Relationships:

Professional language helps build strong relationships with colleagues, superiors, and clients. By using respectful and courteous language, individuals can foster trust and credibility in their interactions. This, in turn, contributes to better teamwork, increased job satisfaction, and long-term professional relationships.

c. Avoiding Misunderstandings:

Clear and polite communication minimizes the risk of misunderstandings and conflicts in the workplace. Using professional language ensures that messages are conveyed accurately and effectively, reducing the chances of misinterpretation or miscommunication. This leads to smoother collaboration and improved efficiency in work processes.

d. Enhancing Professional Image:

Polite and professional language reflects positively on an individual's professional image. It demonstrates a high level of professionalism, character, and communication skills, which are essential in building credibility and authority in the workplace. Employers and clients are more likely to trust and respect individuals who communicate in a polite and professional manner.

e. Resolving Conflicts Amicably:

Inevitably, conflicts may arise in the workplace due to differing opinions, preferences, or personalities. Polite and professional language can help individuals address conflicts in a constructive and respectful manner. By maintaining a courteous tone and using diplomatic language, employees can work towards resolving disagreements amicably and preserving working relationships.

2. Examples of Polite and Professional Language in the Office:

Now, let's explore some examples of how polite and professional language can be applied in various workplace scenarios:

a. Greeting and Welcoming Colleagues:
   - Polite: "Good morning, [Colleague's Name]. I hope you're doing well today."
   - Professional: "Hello, [Colleague's Name]. It's good to see you. How can I assist you today?"

b. Requesting Assistance or Information:
   - Polite: "Would you mind helping me with this task when you have a moment?"
   - Professional: "I would appreciate your expertise on this matter. Could you provide some guidance?"

c. Giving Feedback or Constructive Criticism:
   - Polite: "I appreciate your effort on this project. Perhaps we can explore some areas for improvement together."
   - Professional: "Your work is valuable, and I believe we can enhance it further by focusing on specific aspects."

d. Expressing Gratitude and Recognition:
- Polite: "Thank you for your hard work and dedication to the team. It doesn't go unnoticed."
- Professional: "I commend you for your outstanding contribution to the project. Your commitment is truly appreciated."

e. Apologizing for Mistakes or Misunderstandings:
- Polite: "I apologize for any inconvenience caused. Let's work together to resolve this issue."
- Professional: "I take full responsibility for the oversight. I am committed to rectifying the situation promptly."

f. Declining Requests or Managing Expectations:
- Polite: "I'm unable to accommodate that request at this moment. Is there an alternative solution we could explore?"
- Professional: "Based on our current workload, I recommend prioritizing other tasks. Let's discuss a revised timeline."

g. Handling Difficult Conversations or Conflicts:
- Polite: "I understand your perspective, and I believe we can find a mutually beneficial solution through open dialogue."
- Professional: "Let's address the issue constructively and collaboratively to ensure a positive outcome for all parties involved."

h. Communicating with Clients or External Stakeholders:
- Polite: "Thank you for considering our services. We look forward to supporting your needs."
- Professional: "We are committed to delivering exceptional service to meet your requirements. Please let us know how we can assist you further."

3. Strategies for Improving Polite and Professional Language in the Office:

To enhance the use of polite and professional language in the workplace, individuals can adopt the following strategies:

a. Active Listening:
Effective communication starts with active listening. By listening attentively to others' perspectives and inputs, individuals can respond thoughtfully and respectfully. This demonstrates empathy and understanding, leading to more positive interactions.

b. Use of Positive Language:
Choosing positive language can help maintain a friendly and encouraging tone in conversations. By using phrases like "thank you," "please," and "I appreciate," individuals can express gratitude and positivity in their interactions.

c. Tone and Body Language:
In addition to verbal communication, non-verbal cues such as tone of voice and body language play a crucial role in conveying politeness and professionalism. Maintaining a calm and composed demeanor, making eye contact, and using a moderate tone can enhance the effectiveness of communication.

d. Empathy and Respect:
It is important to show empathy and respect towards others' feelings and opinions. Acknowledging different perspectives and treating colleagues with respect fosters a culture of inclusivity and understanding in the workplace.

e. Conflict Resolution Skills:

When conflicts arise, individuals should approach them with a problem-solving mindset. By actively listening, communicating assertively yet respectfully, and exploring compromises, employees can resolve conflicts constructively while maintaining a professional demeanor.

f. Continuous Learning and Feedback:

Seeking feedback from colleagues and superiors can help individuals improve their communication skills. Engaging in professional development opportunities, such as communication workshops or training sessions, can also enhance one's ability to communicate politely and professionally.

4. Impact of Polite and Professional Language on Organizational Culture:

The use of polite and professional language in the office has a significant impact on shaping the organizational culture. When employees consistently communicate with respect and professionalism, it creates a culture of collaboration, trust, and mutual respect. Here are some ways in which polite and professional language influences organizational culture:

a. Trust and Credibility:

Polite and professional communication builds trust and credibility within the organization. When employees interact respectfully and courteously, it fosters a culture of transparency and reliability. This, in turn, strengthens working relationships and enhances teamwork.

b. Employee Engagement and Morale:

A culture of polite and professional communication promotes employee engagement and morale. When individuals feel respected and valued in their interactions, they are more likely to be motivated, productive, and satisfied in their roles. This contributes to a positive work environment and boosts overall morale within the organization.

c. Team Collaboration and Productivity:

Effective communication through polite and professional language facilitates seamless collaboration among team members. By communicating clearly, respectfully, and professionally, employees can work together more efficiently, share ideas effectively, and achieve common goals. This leads to increased productivity and better outcomes for the organization.

d. Conflict Resolution and Problem-Solving:

A culture of professional communication enables employees to address conflicts and challenges effectively. When individuals approach disagreements with respect and diplomacy, they can work towards solutions collaboratively and avoid escalating conflicts. This promotes a culture of constructive problem-solving and continuous improvement within the organization.

e. Customer Satisfaction and Brand Reputation:

Polite and professional communication extends beyond internal interactions to interactions with clients and external stakeholders. By maintaining a professional demeanor and using courteous language when engaging with customers, employees can enhance customer satisfaction and contribute to a positive brand reputation. This, in turn, cultivates loyalty and trust among clients, leading to long-term business success.

5. Challenges in Maintaining Polite and Professional Language:

While using polite and professional language is beneficial in the workplace, there are challenges that individuals may encounter when striving to maintain a high standard of communication. Some common challenges include:

a. Emotional Reactions:
Emotions can sometimes cloud judgment and lead to unprofessional communication. When individuals are under stress, feeling frustrated, or experiencing personal issues, it can be challenging to maintain a polite and professional demeanor in interactions. Learning to manage emotions effectively is crucial for overcoming this challenge.

b. Cultural and Language Differences:
In diverse work environments, cultural and language differences can pose challenges in communication. Misunderstandings may arise due to varying cultural norms, communication styles, or language barriers. It is important for individuals to be mindful of these differences and adapt their communication to ensure clarity and respect for cultural diversity.

c. Hierarchical Structures:
In organizations with hierarchical structures, there may be challenges in maintaining polite and professional language across different levels of authority. Employees may feel intimidated or hesitant to communicate openly with superiors, leading to a breakdown in effective communication. Establishing

open channels of communication and promoting a culture of mutual respect can help address this challenge.

d. Remote Work and Virtual Communication:

With the rise of remote work and virtual communication, maintaining polite and professional language in digital interactions can be challenging. The lack of face-to-face communication can make it harder to convey tone and non-verbal cues effectively. Individuals need to be mindful of their written communication and use clear, respectful language in virtual interactions to avoid misunderstandings.

e. Time Constraints and Workload Pressures:

In fast-paced work environments with tight deadlines and high workloads, employees may struggle to maintain polite and professional language under pressure. Stress and time constraints can lead to abrupt or curt communication, affecting the quality of interactions. Practicing mindfulness, prioritizing effective communication, and managing workload effectively can help individuals navigate this challenge.

6. Strategies for Overcoming Challenges in Using Polite and Professional Language:

Despite the challenges that individuals may face in maintaining polite and professional language in the office, there are strategies they can employ to overcome these obstacles:

a. Self-awareness:

Developing self-awareness is key to overcoming challenges in communication. By recognizing one's emotions, triggers, and communication patterns, individuals can better regulate their responses and adapt their communication style to fit the situation.

b. Training and Development:

Engaging in communication training and development programs can help individuals enhance their communication skills. Workshops on active listening, conflict resolution, cultural competence, and emotional intelligence can provide valuable tools and strategies for improving communication in the workplace.

c. Peer Mentoring and Feedback:

Seeking feedback from peers, mentors, or colleagues can offer valuable insights into one's communication style and areas for improvement. Engaging in peer mentoring relationships can provide support, guidance, and constructive feedback to help individuals navigate communication challenges effectively.

d. Mindfulness and Stress Management:

Practicing mindfulness techniques and stress management strategies can help individuals maintain composure and professionalism in challenging situations. By managing stress effectively, employees can approach communication with a clear and focused mindset, reducing the likelihood of impulsive or unprofessional behavior.

e. Regular Reflection and Improvement:

Taking time for self-reflection and continuous improvement is essential for enhancing communication skills. Individuals can reflect on their interactions, identify areas for growth, and set goals for improving their communication style over time.

Regular feedback loops and self-assessment can aid in ongoing development.

7. Conclusion:

In conclusion, polite and professional language is a cornerstone of effective communication in the workplace. By using respectful, courteous, and professional language, individuals can foster a positive work environment, build strong relationships, avoid misunderstandings, and enhance their professional image. Polite and professional communication contributes to a culture of trust, collaboration, and respect within organizations, leading to improved employee engagement, customer satisfaction, and overall organizational success.

Employing strategies such as active listening, positive language use, empathy, conflict resolution skills, and continuous learning can help individuals enhance their communication skills and maintain a high standard of polite and professional language in the office. While challenges such as emotional reactions, cultural differences, hierarchical structures, remote work, and workload pressures may arise, individuals can overcome these obstacles by practicing self-awareness, seeking training and feedback, managing stress effectively, and engaging in regular reflection and improvement.

Ultimately, by prioritizing polite and professional language in their interactions, employees can contribute to a positive workplace culture, effective teamwork, and successful business outcomes. Embracing the value of respectful and professional communication is not just a matter of etiquette; it is a fundamental aspect of building strong relationships, fostering collaboration, and achieving excellence in the modern workplace.

7

Handling Common Workplace Situations

In today's dynamic work environment, professionals encounter a wide range of situations that require adept handling to navigate successfully. From conflicts with colleagues to managing deadlines and dealing with difficult clients, employees must be equipped with the skills and strategies to address these challenges effectively. This deep dive will explore common workplace situations and provide detailed explanations, examples, and best practices for handling them.

1. Conflict Resolution:

Conflicts are inevitable in any workplace due to differences in personalities, work styles, and perspectives. Effective conflict resolution is crucial to maintain a positive work environment and foster productive relationships. Here are some strategies for handling conflicts:

- Active Listening: When resolving conflicts, it's essential to listen actively to the other party's concerns without interrupting.

For example, if two team members are arguing over project responsibilities, a manager can practice active listening by paraphrasing each person's viewpoint to demonstrate understanding.

- Seeking a Win-Win Solution: Encouraging parties to focus on common interests and goals rather than positions can help achieve a mutually beneficial outcome. For instance, in a conflict between a marketing and sales team over campaign strategies, a compromise that addresses both teams' objectives may be reached by emphasizing shared business objectives.

- Mediation: In cases where conflicts escalate and parties are unable to find a resolution on their own, involving a neutral mediator can facilitate productive discussions and guide the parties toward a mutually acceptable solution.

2. Handling Difficult Clients:

Dealing with challenging clients is a common occurrence in many industries, including customer service, sales, and consulting. Professionals must effectively manage these situations to uphold the organization's reputation and ensure client satisfaction. Here are some tips for handling difficult clients:

- Maintain Calm and Professionalism: When faced with an irate client, it's crucial to remain composed and respond in a calm and professional manner. For example, a customer service representative dealing with a dissatisfied customer can acknowledge their concerns and empathize with their frustration before proposing solutions.

- Set Clear Boundaries: Establishing clear boundaries and communicating expectations can help manage difficult clients' behavior. For instance, a project manager working with a demanding client can set realistic timelines and scope of work upfront to avoid misunderstandings.

- Involve Higher Management if Necessary: In cases where a client's demands are unreasonable or conflicts persist, involving higher management or escalating the issue to a designated escalation point can help address the situation effectively.

3. Performance Feedback and Improvement:
   Providing and receiving feedback is an integral part of professional growth and development. Constructive feedback helps employees understand their strengths and areas for improvement, contributing to enhanced performance and job satisfaction. Here's how to handle performance feedback effectively:

- Timely and Specific Feedback: Providing feedback in a timely manner and specifying areas of improvement helps employees understand expectations and take actionable steps toward better performance. For example, a manager can provide specific feedback on a team member's presentation skills after a client meeting, highlighting both strengths and areas for improvement.

- Focus on Behavior and Results: When delivering feedback, it's essential to focus on observable behavior and outcomes rather than making subjective judgments. This ensures that feedback is objective and actionable for the recipient.

- Encourage Two-Way Communication: Creating a culture of open communication where employees feel comfortable providing feedback to their managers fosters a collaborative and supportive work environment conducive to continuous improvement.

4. Meeting Deadlines and Managing Workload:

Meeting deadlines and effectively managing workload are critical skills for professional success. In fast-paced work environments, employees must prioritize tasks, set realistic timelines, and adapt to changing priorities to ensure timely delivery of projects. Here's how to handle deadlines and workload management:

- Prioritize Tasks: Identifying high-priority tasks and allocating time and resources accordingly helps employees focus on critical deliverables and meet deadlines effectively. For instance, using a priority matrix to categorize tasks based on urgency and importance can guide decision-making on task allocation.

- Set Realistic Deadlines: Setting realistic deadlines based on task complexity, available resources, and potential barriers ensures that expectations are aligned with achievable outcomes. Collaborating with team members to set collective deadlines can help distribute workload effectively and prevent bottlenecks.

- Utilize Time Management Tools: Leveraging time management tools and techniques, such as to-do lists, calendars, and project management software, can aid in organizing tasks, tracking progress, and managing time effectively to meet deadlines.

5. Effective Communication in the Workplace:

Communication lies at the heart of successful collaboration, decision-making, and relationship-building in the workplace. Clear and transparent communication ensures that information is conveyed accurately and understood by all stakeholders. Here are some strategies for effective workplace communication:

- Use Active Listening: Active listening involves fully concentrating, understanding, responding, and remembering what is said during communication. By actively listening to colleagues, employees can avoid misunderstandings and demonstrate respect for their viewpoints.

- Choose the Right Communication Channel: Selecting the appropriate communication channel based on the message's nature, urgency, and audience can enhance communication efficiency. For example, urgent matters may require a face-to-face discussion, while routine updates can be communicated via email.

- Provide Constructive Feedback: Offering constructive feedback that is specific, behavior-focused, and actionable helps improve performance and build stronger relationships among team members. Constructive feedback should highlight both areas of strength and areas for improvement to facilitate professional growth.

6. Managing Remote Teams:

With the rise of remote work, many professionals find themselves leading or working in virtual teams dispersed across different locations. Managing remote teams effectively requires leveraging technology, fostering collaboration, and maintaining clear communication channels. Here's how to handle managing remote teams:

- Establish Clear Expectations: Clearly defining roles, responsibilities, and expectations for remote team members helps ensure alignment and accountability. Setting agreed-upon communication protocols and work schedules enables team members to know what is expected of them.

- Utilize Collaboration Tools: Leveraging collaboration tools such as project management software, video conferencing platforms, and messaging apps can facilitate seamless communication and coordination among remote team members. Tools like Trello, Slack, and Zoom help streamline workflow and keep team members connected.

- Encourage Team Building Activities: Organizing virtual team building activities, such as virtual happy hours, online games, or team challenges, helps strengthen relationships and boost team morale among remote employees.

7. Personal Development and Career Growth:

Investing in personal development and pursuing career growth opportunities are essential for professionals looking to advance their careers and reach their full potential. Continuous learning, skills enhancement, and networking play a crucial role in career progression. Here's how to handle personal development and career growth:

- Set SMART Goals: Establishing SMART (Specific, Measurable,

Achievable, Relevant, Time-bound) goals for personal and professional development provides a clear roadmap for growth and progress. By defining specific objectives and timelines, employees can track their achievements and make necessary adjustments.

- Seek Mentorship and Coaching: Engaging with mentors, coaches, or industry experts can offer valuable guidance, feedback, and support for career advancement. Mentors provide insights based on their experience, helping mentees navigate challenges and make informed career decisions.

- Attend Training and Development Programs: Participating in training programs, workshops, seminars, and online courses tailored to employees' needs and career goals enhances skills, knowledge, and expertise, contributing to professional development and career growth.

8. Adapting to Change and Uncertainty:

In today's rapidly evolving business landscape, professionals must adapt to change and uncertainty to stay resilient and thrive in the face of challenges. Adaptable employees can effectively navigate transitions, embrace new opportunities, and pivot in response to emerging trends. Here's how to handle change and uncertainty in the workplace:

- Cultivate a Growth Mindset: Embracing a growth mindset, which entails a belief in one's ability to learn and grow through challenges, fosters resilience and adaptability in the face of change. By viewing setbacks as learning opportunities, employees can approach change with a positive and proactive mindset.

- Communicate Transparently: Transparent communication from leadership about organizational changes, challenges, and future plans helps employees understand the reasons behind change and reduces uncertainty. Providing context and updates on changes can alleviate anxiety and foster trust among team members.

- Embrace Innovation: Encouraging a culture of innovation and experimentation within the organization empowers employees to generate creative solutions, adapt to changing circumstances, and drive continuous improvement. By embracing innovation, employees can navigate uncertainty and capitalize on emerging opportunities.

In conclusion, handling common workplace situations effectively requires a combination of emotional intelligence, communication skills, adaptability, and problem-solving abilities. By applying the strategies and best practices outlined above, professionals can navigate conflicts, manage workload, communicate effectively, and achieve personal and career growth in today's diverse and dynamic work environments. Continuous learning, self-reflection, and a proactive approach to handling workplace challenges are essential for professional success and fulfillment.

8

Using Email and Written Communication Effectively

Email and written communication play a crucial role in our personal and professional lives. In today's digital age, the ability to craft clear, concise, and effective written messages is more important than ever. Whether you are drafting an email to a colleague, creating a report for your boss, or composing a letter to a client, mastering the art of written communication can help you convey your message with clarity and professionalism.

Effective written communication is essential for several reasons. First and foremost, clear and concise written messages help ensure that your intended message is understood by the recipient. Miscommunication can lead to confusion, errors, and misunderstandings, which can have a negative impact on your relationships and work performance. By carefully crafting your written messages, you can reduce the likelihood of misunderstandings and ensure that your message is received as intended.

Another reason why effective written communication is important is that it reflects your professionalism and attention to detail. When you take the time to carefully draft and edit your written messages, you demonstrate that you care about the quality of your work and the impression you make on others. Whether you are communicating with colleagues, clients, or supervisors, presenting yourself as a competent and thoughtful communicator can help you build trust and credibility in your professional relationships.

In this guide, we will explore the key principles of effective email and written communication and provide practical tips and examples to help you improve your communication skills.

1. Understand Your Audience

One of the most important aspects of effective communication is understanding your audience. Before you begin drafting an email or written message, take some time to consider who will be reading it and what their needs, preferences, and expectations are. Tailoring your message to your audience can help ensure that your message resonates with them and achieves the desired outcome.

For example, if you are writing an email to a colleague, you can consider their communication style, level of familiarity with the topic, and preferred level of formality. By adapting your message to suit your colleague's preferences, you can create a more engaging and effective communication experience.

2. Be Clear and Concise

Clarity and conciseness are key elements of effective written communication. When crafting an email or written message, aim to convey your message in a clear and straightforward manner. Avoid using jargon, complex language, or unnecessary details that can confuse your reader. Instead, focus on communicating your main points concisely and directly.

For example, instead of writing a lengthy email with multiple paragraphs of background information, get straight to the point by outlining your key message in the first few sentences. By being clear and concise, you can make it easier for your reader to understand and respond to your message.

3. Use Proper Formatting and Structure

Proper formatting and structure can help make your written messages more readable and engaging. When composing an email or written document, consider using headings, bullet points, and numbered lists to organize your content and make it easier to digest. Breaking up your text into smaller sections can also help improve readability and draw attention to key points.

For example, if you are writing a report for your team, you can use headings to separate different sections of the report, such as the introduction, key findings, and recommendations. By using headings and subheadings, you can create a clear and structured document that guides your reader through the content.

4. Proofread and Edit Your Work

Before sending an email or written message, always take the time to proofread and edit your work. Typos, grammatical errors, and spelling mistakes can detract from the professionalism of your message and make it more difficult for your reader to understand your intended meaning. By reviewing your work carefully, you can catch and correct any errors before sending your message.

For example, after drafting an email, take a few minutes to review it for spelling and grammatical errors. You can also read your message out loud to ensure that it flows smoothly and conveys your message effectively. By proofreading and editing your work, you can make sure that your written communication is clear, polished, and professional.

5. Be Mindful of Tone and Politeness

The tone and politeness of your written messages can have a significant impact on how they are received by the recipient. When composing an email or written communication, be mindful of your tone and strive to maintain a respectful and professional demeanor. Avoid using language that is overly casual, abrasive, or confrontational, as it can create a negative impression and damage your relationships with others.

For example, when providing feedback to a colleague, focus on using constructive and supportive language to help them improve their performance. By being mindful of your tone and politeness, you can foster positive and effective communication with your colleagues, clients, and superiors.

6. Use Appropriate Subject Lines

The subject line of an email is one of the first things that your recipient will see, so it is important to use it effectively to capture their attention and convey the purpose of your message. When drafting an email, choose a clear and descriptive subject line that summarizes the main topic or action required. Avoid using vague or overly generic subject lines that can confuse or mislead your reader.

For example, if you are requesting feedback on a project from your team, you can use a subject line like "Request for Feedback on Project XYZ" to clearly indicate the purpose of your email. By using an appropriate subject line, you can help your recipient quickly understand the content and importance of your message.

7. Respond in a Timely Manner

Timely responses are essential for effective email and written communication. When you receive an email or written message, make it a priority to reply promptly, even if it is just to acknowledge receipt of the message. Delayed responses can create frustration and uncertainty for the sender, leading to communication breakdowns and misunderstandings.

For example, if you receive an email from a client requesting information, try to respond within 24 hours to demonstrate your responsiveness and commitment to meeting their needs. By responding in a timely manner, you can build trust and credibility with your clients and colleagues.

8. Use Professional Signatures

Your email signature is an important part of your written communication, as it provides essential contact information and helps establish your professional identity. When creating an email signature, include your full name, job title, company name, contact information, and any relevant links or social media profiles. A professional email signature can help you make a positive impression on your recipients and provide them with the information they need to contact you easily.

For example, your email signature can look like this:

[Full Name]
   [Job Title]
   [Company Name]
   [Phone Number]
   [Email Address]
   [Website]
   [LinkedIn Profile]

By using a professional email signature, you can enhance the credibility and professionalism of your written communication and make it easier for recipients to engage with you.

In conclusion, mastering the art of effective email and written communication is an essential skill that can help you communicate with clarity, professionalism, and impact. By understanding your audience, being clear and concise, using proper formatting and structure, proofreading and editing your work, being mindful of tone and politeness, using appropriate subject lines, responding in a timely manner, and using professional signatures, you can enhance your written communication skills and build stronger relationships with your colleagues, clients, and stakeholders. Remember that effective written communication is a continuous learning process, so take the time to practice and refine your skills to become a more confident and effective communicator in both your personal and professional life.

9

Practicing English Conversations at Work

Practicing English conversations at work is a crucial skill that can greatly benefit individuals in various professional settings. In today's globalized world, the ability to communicate effectively in English has become an essential skill for many workplaces. Whether you work in a multinational company, a start-up, or a small local business with international clients, being able to converse fluently and confidently in English can open up a world of opportunities for you. This article will explore the importance of practicing English conversations at work, provide tips for improving your English communication skills, and offer examples to help you apply these tips in real-life scenarios.

Importance of Practicing English Conversations at Work:

1. Enhances Communication Skills: Practicing English conversations at work is a great way to enhance your overall communication skills. Effective communication is key to building

strong relationships with colleagues, clients, and superiors. By improving your English conversational skills, you can convey your ideas clearly, express your thoughts effectively, and engage in meaningful discussions that contribute to the success of your team and organization.

2. Boosts Confidence: Engaging in English conversations at work can boost your confidence and self-esteem. Confidence is a fundamental trait that can help you excel in your career. When you feel comfortable speaking in English and expressing yourself with ease, you are more likely to take on new challenges, participate in meetings, and take initiative in projects. Confidence in your English communication skills can also help you build credibility and create a positive impression in the workplace.

3. Facilitates Collaboration: Effective communication is essential for successful collaboration in the workplace. Practicing English conversations with your colleagues enables you to work together more efficiently, exchange ideas, provide feedback constructively, and resolve conflicts smoothly. By improving your English conversational skills, you can enhance teamwork, promote creativity, and achieve collective goals with greater ease.

4. Expands Professional Network: In today's interconnected world, networking plays a vital role in advancing your career. Practicing English conversations at work allows you to connect with professionals from diverse backgrounds, cultures, and regions. Building a strong professional network through English communication can open up new opportunities for career

growth, mentorship, collaboration, and knowledge sharing.

5. Demonstrates Language Proficiency: Demonstrating proficiency in English conversations at work showcases your language skills and reflects your commitment to personal and professional development. Employers value employees who can communicate effectively in English, as it demonstrates adaptability, cultural awareness, and a global mindset. By practicing English conversations regularly, you can establish yourself as a competent and versatile professional in your organization.

Tips for Improving English Conversational Skills at Work:

1. Practice Regularly: The key to improving your English conversational skills is consistent practice. Make an effort to engage in English conversations with your colleagues, attend meetings in English, and participate in discussions or presentations. The more you practice speaking in English, the more comfortable and fluent you will become over time.

2. Expand Your Vocabulary: Building a strong vocabulary is essential for effective communication. Take the initiative to learn new words and phrases related to your industry or field of work. Keep a vocabulary journal, use word-of-the-day apps, and incorporate new terms into your daily conversations to enhance your language proficiency.

3. Listen Actively: Active listening is a crucial component of successful communication. Pay close attention to the speaker's words, tone, and body language during English conversations.

Practice summarizing, paraphrasing, and asking clarifying questions to demonstrate your comprehension and engage effectively in the discussion.

4. Seek Feedback: Don't be afraid to seek feedback from your colleagues or supervisors on your English communication skills. Constructive feedback can help you identify areas for improvement, address any language barriers, and refine your conversational style. Act on the feedback received and incorporate it into your practice sessions to enhance your proficiency.

5. Use English in Daily Tasks: Incorporate English into your daily work routines to develop fluency and confidence. Write emails, reports, or memos in English, attend English language workshops or seminars, and participate in team-building activities that require English communication. By immersing yourself in English communication, you can accelerate your learning and adaptability in the workplace.

6. Role-Play Scenarios: Engaging in role-play scenarios can be an effective way to practice English conversations in different workplace situations. Create role-playing exercises with your colleagues to simulate real-life interactions such as customer inquiries, presentations, negotiations, or team discussions. This hands-on approach can help you apply your language skills in practical settings and improve your communication abilities.

7. Use Language Learning Apps: Take advantage of language learning apps and tools to supplement your English conversational practice. Apps such as Duolingo, Babbel, or Rosetta Stone offer interactive exercises, quizzes, and lessons to help you

enhance your vocabulary, grammar, and pronunciation skills. Set aside time each day to practice with these apps to reinforce your learning and progress.

8. Engage in Social Activities: Participating in social activities outside of work can also be a fun and effective way to practice English conversations. Join English language clubs, discussion groups, or networking events in your community to connect with native speakers and fellow learners. Engaging in informal conversations in a relaxed setting can boost your confidence and fluency in English.

9. Stay Updated: Stay informed about current events, industry trends, and global affairs to broaden your knowledge and improve your conversational skills. Read English newspapers, magazines, or online publications, watch English-language TV shows or podcasts, and follow English-speaking influencers on social media. Being well-informed will not only enhance your language proficiency but also enable you to engage in meaningful conversations on a wide range of topics.

10. Be Patient and Persistent: Improving your English conversational skills takes time and effort, so be patient with yourself and stay persistent in your practice. Set realistic goals, track your progress, and celebrate your achievements along the way. Remember that language learning is a gradual process, and with dedication and perseverance, you can continue to sharpen your English communication skills and excel in your professional endeavors.

Examples of English Conversations at Work:

1. Participating in a Team Meeting:

Scenario:
You are a project manager leading a team meeting to discuss the progress of a new product launch. Your team members are from different departments, and the meeting is conducted in English to ensure clear communication and alignment.

Example Conversation:
Project Manager: Good morning, everyone. Thank you for joining today's meeting. Let's start by reviewing the milestones we have achieved so far in the product development phase.

Marketing Specialist: Sure, I'll provide an update on the marketing campaign progress. We have finalized the target audience analysis and are now working on the creative assets for the launch.

Finance Analyst: From a financial perspective, we have estimated the budget requirements for the promotional activities and are monitoring the cost projections against the allocated funds.

Project Manager: Great to hear about the progress. Let's discuss any challenges or roadblocks that require immediate attention to ensure we stay on track for the launch deadline.

2. Conducting a Performance Review:

Scenario:
As a team leader, you are conducting a performance review

with one of your direct reports to provide feedback on their recent projects and set goals for their professional development. The review is conducted in English to facilitate a transparent and constructive conversation.

Example Conversation:

Team Leader: Hello, Sarah. I appreciate you taking the time for this performance review meeting. I wanted to discuss your recent projects and gather your feedback on the outcomes.

Sarah: Thank you, I'm looking forward to discussing my progress and areas for improvement. I completed the marketing campaign for the new product line and received positive feedback from the client.

Team Leader: That's great to hear. Your creativity and attention to detail were evident in the campaign execution. Moving forward, I recommend focusing on developing your project management skills to enhance efficiency and meet project deadlines consistently.

Sarah: I appreciate the feedback. I will work on improving my time management and prioritization skills to deliver projects more effectively in the future.

3. Resolving a Conflict in a Team Discussion:

Scenario:

During a team discussion on project strategies, two team members have differing opinions on the approach to a critical task. As a facilitator, you need to mediate the conflict and guide the team towards a consensus. The conversation is conducted in English to ensure transparent communication and alignment.

Example Conversation:
Facilitator: Let's address the differing opinions on the implementation approach for the customer engagement strategy. Anna, could you share your perspective on the proposed approach?

Anna: I believe that focusing on social media marketing would yield higher engagement rates among our target audience and drive brand visibility effectively.

John: While I agree that social media marketing is important, I suggest incorporating email marketing campaigns to reach a wider audience and personalize the communication with our customers.

Facilitator: Both perspectives have their merits. Let's explore a hybrid approach that combines the strengths of both strategies to maximize our impact. Anna, could you provide insights on how we can integrate social media and email marketing for the campaign?

By practicing English conversations in various workplace scenarios such as team meetings, performance reviews, and conflict resolutions, individuals can develop their language skills, enhance their communication effectiveness, and build stronger professional relationships.

In conclusion, practicing English conversations at work is a valuable skill that can benefit individuals in their professional development and career advancement. By improving their English communication skills, professionals can enhance their ability to collaborate, network, and succeed in diverse work environments. Through consistent practice, active listening, seeking feedback, and engaging in real-life scenarios, individuals can refine their language proficiency, boost their confidence, and demonstrate their communication capabilities effectively. By implementing the tips and examples provided in this article, individuals can elevate their English conversational skills and thrive in their professional endeavors.

10

Overcoming Communication Challenges

Communication is an essential aspect of human interaction that plays a crucial role in both personal and professional relationships. Effective communication helps in fostering understanding, building trust, resolving conflicts, and achieving common goals. However, various challenges can hinder successful communication, leading to misunderstandings, frustration, and conflict. These challenges can arise from different sources such as differences in cultural backgrounds, language barriers, emotional barriers, noise, lack of feedback, and more. Overcoming these challenges is crucial to maintaining healthy relationships and ensuring successful outcomes in various aspects of life.

One of the important communication challenges faced by individuals and organizations is overcoming cultural differences. People from different cultural backgrounds may have distinct communication styles, norms, values, and beliefs that can impact how messages are sent and received. For example, in some cultures, direct communication is valued, while in others, indirect communication is preferred. This cultural variation can lead to misunderstandings, misconceptions, and conflicts if not addressed appropriately.

To overcome cultural communication challenges, individuals need to develop cultural intelligence and sensitivity to understand and respect the cultural differences of others. This involves being open-minded, empathetic, and willing to adapt communication styles to accommodate diverse cultural perspectives. By practicing active listening, seeking clarification, and being respectful of cultural differences, individuals can bridge the gap and foster effective communication across cultures.

Language barriers also pose a significant challenge to effective communication, especially in multicultural and multilingual settings. Misinterpretations, misunderstandings, and miscommunication can occur when individuals do not speak the same language or have limited proficiency in a particular language. This can lead to confusion, frustration, and breakdowns in communication that hinder collaboration and productivity.

To overcome language barriers, individuals can employ various strategies such as using interpreters or translation services, simplifying language when speaking to non-native speakers, and practicing patience and understanding when communicating with individuals who speak different languages. Learning basic phrases in different languages, using visual aids, and using body language and gestures can also help overcome language barriers and facilitate effective communication across language boundaries.

Emotional barriers are another common communication challenge that can affect the quality of interactions between individuals. Emotional barriers such as anger, fear, stress, and lack of trust can hinder effective communication by clouding judgment, creating conflicts, and impeding the exchange of ideas and information.

To overcome emotional barriers in communication, individuals need to cultivate self-awareness, emotional intelligence, and empathy. By recognizing and managing their own emotions effectively, individuals can communicate more clearly, openly, and respectfully with others. Active listening, acknowledging emotions, and validating others' feelings can help foster trust, build rapport, and overcome emotional barriers in communication.

Noise and distractions in the communication environment can also create challenges for effective communication. External factors such as loud noises, interruptions, technological glitches, and environmental distractions can interfere with the transmission and reception of messages, leading to miscommunication and misunderstandings.

To overcome noise and distractions in communication, individuals can create a conducive communication environment by minimizing distractions, choosing a quiet and private space for conversations, using communication tools and technologies effectively, and practicing active listening skills to focus on the message being communicated. By eliminating or reducing external noise and distractions, individuals can enhance the clarity and effectiveness of communication interactions.

Another common communication challenge is the lack of feedback or feedback mismatch, where individuals do not receive timely, constructive, or accurate feedback on their messages. Without feedback, individuals may not know if their messages have been understood, if their ideas have been accepted, or if adjustments are needed to improve communication effectiveness.

To overcome the challenge of feedback in communication, individuals can actively seek feedback from others, ask clarifying questions, and encourage open and honest communication to ensure that messages are received and understood correctly. Providing specific, constructive feedback to others and being receptive to feedback can help improve communication effectiveness and address any misunderstandings or gaps in communication.

In conclusion, overcoming communication challenges is essential for fostering effective relationships, resolving conflicts, and achieving successful outcomes in personal and professional settings. By recognizing and addressing challenges such as cultural differences, language barriers, emotional barriers, noise and distractions, and feedback issues, individuals can enhance their communication skills and build stronger connections with others. By practicing empathy, active listening, adaptability, and openness to feedback, individuals can navigate through communication challenges and create more meaningful and impactful interactions in various contexts.

11

Building Connections and Networking in English

Building Connections and Networking in English is a fundamental aspect of personal and professional growth. It involves establishing and nurturing relationships with individuals to exchange ideas, information, and opportunities. In today's interconnected world, networking plays a crucial role in career advancement, business development, and personal enrichment. This essay will delve deeply into the importance of building connections, strategies for effective networking, the benefits it offers, and provide real-world examples to illustrate these concepts.

Importance of Building Connections and Networking

Building connections and networking is essential for both personal and professional success. It allows individuals to expand their knowledge, widen their perspective, and open doors to new opportunities. In business, effective networking can lead to partnerships, collaborations, and increased visibility in the industry. For job seekers, networking can be the key to discovering hidden job opportunities and securing employment. Moreover, building connections helps in establishing a support system, gaining mentors, and receiving guidance from experienced individuals.

1. Career Advancement: Networking is crucial for career growth. By connecting with professionals in your field, you can learn about job openings, industry trends, and skill requirements. Networking also provides access to mentors who can offer guidance and support in navigating your career path. For example, attending industry events and conferences can help you meet influential people who may open doors to new job opportunities or collaborations.

2. Knowledge Exchange: Networking provides opportunities to learn from others with different perspectives and expertise. By connecting with individuals from diverse backgrounds, you can gain insights into new technologies, trends, and best practices. For instance, participating in online forums or joining professional associations can help you stay updated on the latest developments in your industry.

3. Business Development: For entrepreneurs and business owners, networking is essential for growth and sustainability. By building relationships with potential clients, partners, and investors, you can expand your customer base, explore new markets, and gain valuable feedback on your products or services. Networking events, such as trade shows or business mixers, offer platforms to showcase your offerings and connect with potential business collaborators.

4. Personal Enrichment: Networking goes beyond professional benefits and also enhances personal growth. By interacting with individuals from diverse backgrounds, you can broaden your horizons, develop cultural intelligence, and build empathy. Networking can also lead to lifelong friendships, providing emotional support and companionship in both good and challenging times.

Strategies for Effective Networking

Effective networking requires a strategic approach and a genuine interest in building relationships. Here are some strategies to help you maximize your networking efforts:

1. Set Clear Goals: Before attending networking events or reaching out to new contacts, define your objectives. Whether you are looking for job opportunities, seeking mentorship, or exploring collaboration prospects, having clear goals will guide your networking efforts and help you focus on relevant connections.

2. Build a Strong Online Presence: In today's digital age, online networking is as important as in-person interactions. Maintain an updated and professional presence on social media platforms like LinkedIn, where you can showcase your skills, connect with industry professionals, and engage in meaningful conversations.

3. Attend Networking Events: Make an effort to attend industry conferences, seminars, workshops, and networking mixers. These events provide valuable opportunities to meet new peo-

ple, exchange ideas, and build connections with like-minded professionals. Remember to bring your business cards and be prepared to introduce yourself concisely.

4. Follow Up: Networking does not end after the initial introduction. Follow up with your new contacts by sending a personalized message or email to express your interest in continuing the conversation. Stay in touch with your connections by sharing relevant articles, attending their events, or offering assistance when needed.

5. Offer Value: Networking is not just about what you can gain from others but also about what you can offer in return. Be generous with your knowledge, resources, and time to build mutually beneficial relationships. By providing value to your network, you establish yourself as a reliable and trustworthy partner.

6. Be Authentic and Listen: Authenticity is key to building genuine connections. Be yourself when networking and focus on building meaningful relationships based on trust and respect. Listen actively to your conversation partners, show genuine interest in their stories, and ask insightful questions to deepen the connection.

Benefits of Building Connections and Networking

The benefits of building connections and networking are manifold and extend across various aspects of life and career. Some of the key benefits include:

1. Opportunity for Career Growth: Networking opens doors to new job opportunities, promotions, and career advancements. By connecting with professionals in your industry, you can learn about job openings before they are publicly advertised and gain valuable insights into the skills and qualifications that employers are seeking.

2. Access to Mentorship and Guidance: Through networking, you can establish relationships with experienced professionals who can serve as mentors and provide guidance in your career journey. Mentors offer valuable advice, share their wisdom, and help you navigate challenges and obstacles in your professional life.

3. Increased Visibility and Credibility: Building a strong network enhances your visibility in your industry or community. By connecting with influential individuals and maintaining a positive reputation, you can build credibility and trust among your peers, clients, and collaborators. This visibility can lead to new opportunities and collaborations.

4. Knowledge Expansion: Networking exposes you to diverse perspectives, experiences, and ideas that can broaden your knowledge and understanding of various subjects. By engaging with individuals from different backgrounds and industries, you can stay informed about the latest trends, technologies, and best practices in your field.

5. Enhanced Problem-Solving Abilities: Networking allows you to tap into a diverse pool of expertise and resources when faced with challenges or problems. By reaching out to your

network for advice or solutions, you can benefit from different viewpoints and innovative approaches to problem-solving.

6. Support System and Emotional Wellbeing: Building connections and networking also contribute to your emotional wellbeing by providing a support system of friends, mentors, and colleagues. These relationships offer emotional support, encouragement, and advice during both professional and personal challenges.

Real-World Examples of Effective Networking

To illustrate the importance and impact of networking, let's look at some real-world examples of individuals who have leveraged their connections to achieve success in their respective fields:

1. Sheryl Sandberg, COO of Facebook: Sheryl Sandberg is known for her strategic networking skills, which have played a significant role in her career advancement. She built strong relationships with industry leaders, including Larry Summers and Mark Zuckerberg, which eventually led to her becoming the COO of Facebook. Sandberg's ability to cultivate meaningful connections and leverage her network has been instrumental in her professional success.

2. Richard Branson, Founder of Virgin Group: Richard Branson is a prime example of how effective networking can drive business growth and innovation. Throughout his career, Branson has strategically built relationships with investors, business leaders, and decision-makers, allowing him to expand his Virgin brand across various industries, from music to airlines.

Branson's ability to network with influential individuals has been a key factor in his entrepreneurial success.

3. Malala Yousafzai, Activist and Nobel Laureate: Malala Yousafzai exemplifies how networking can amplify one's impact and influence on a global scale. Despite facing adversity as a young activist advocating for girls' education, Malala leveraged her connections within the education and human rights communities to amplify her message and reach a wider audience. Through her strategic networking efforts, Malala has become a prominent voice for education and social change worldwide.

4. Elon Musk, CEO of Tesla and SpaceX: Elon Musk is renowned for his ability to network strategically and attract top talent to his companies. Musk has cultivated relationships with leading engineers, scientists, and investors, allowing him to recruit top-notch professionals for his ventures, such as Tesla and SpaceX. Musk's expansive network and collaborative approach have been instrumental in driving innovation and achieving success in the competitive tech industry.

These examples demonstrate how building connections and networking can propel individuals to new heights of success, whether in business, advocacy, or innovation. By nurturing relationships, seeking out mentors, and leveraging their networks, these individuals have been able to create impactful change and achieve remarkable accomplishments in their respective fields.

Conclusion

In conclusion, building connections and networking in English is an essential skill that offers numerous benefits for personal and professional growth. By actively engaging with individuals, sharing knowledge, and fostering relationships, you can expand your opportunities, gain valuable insights, and create a supportive community around you. Effective networking requires a strategic approach, authenticity, and a willingness to offer value to others.

Whether you are a job seeker looking for career opportunities, an entrepreneur seeking business partnerships, or an individual looking to expand your knowledge and horizons, networking can open doors to new possibilities and enrich your life in myriad ways. By following the strategies outlined in this essay and learning from real-world examples of successful networkers, you can enhance your networking skills and leverage the power of connections to achieve your goals.

In a world where relationships and collaborations play a crucial role in personal and professional success, investing time and effort in building connections and networking can be a transformative experience that opens up a world of opportunities and enriches your life in ways you never imagined. Embrace networking as a powerful tool for growth, learning, and connection, and witness the profound impact it can have on your journey towards success.

50 Business English Vocabulary with examples:

1. Adept - He is adept at solving complex problems.
2. Agile - To stay competitive, organizations need to be agile in responding to market changes.

3. Benchmark – The company sets a benchmark for quality that others strive to match.

4. Capitalize – We need to capitalize on our strengths to move ahead in the market.

5. Collaboration – Successful projects often result from effective collaboration among team members.

6. Core competency – Developing core competencies can give a company a competitive advantage.

7. Diversification – The company is considering diversification to reduce risk.

8. Efficiency – Improving efficiency can lead to cost savings and increased productivity.

9. Entrepreneur – She is an entrepreneur who has started several successful businesses.

10. Forecast – Based on the latest data, the forecast predicts a downturn in the market.

11. Globalization – Globalization has opened up new markets for many businesses.

12. Incentive – Providing bonuses can be a powerful incentive for employees to work harder.

13. Innovation – Continuous innovation is crucial for staying ahead in the technology industry.

14. Logistics – Good logistics management is essential for timely delivery of products.

15. Marketing strategy – A well-crafted marketing strategy can help a company reach its target audience.

16. Networking – Networking with industry professionals can open up new opportunities.

17. Outsourcing – Many companies outsource certain functions to reduce costs.

18. Partnership – Forming a strategic partnership can help

both companies expand their reach.

19. Quality control - Implementing strict quality control measures ensures that products meet standards.

20. Revenue - The company reported a significant increase in revenue this quarter.

21. Sustainability - Adopting sustainable practices is becoming increasingly important for businesses.

22. Target market - Identifying the target market is crucial for developing effective marketing campaigns.

23. Unprecedented - The pandemic has brought about unprecedented challenges for businesses.

24. Venture - Starting a new venture requires careful planning and consideration.

25. Workforce - The company is investing in training programs to develop its workforce.

26. Acquisition - The acquisition of a rival company can help expand market share.

27. Blue chip - Blue chip companies are known for their stability and strong financial performance.

28. Collateral - The bank required collateral to secure the loan.

29. Depreciation - The company accounts for asset depreciation in its financial statements.

30. Equity - Investors can acquire equity in a company by purchasing shares.

31. Fiscal year - The company's fiscal year ends in December.

32. Gross profit - Calculating gross profit involves subtracting the cost of goods sold from total revenue.

33. Hedge - Companies often use hedging strategies to mitigate financial risks.

34. Inflation - Inflation can erode the purchasing power of a

currency.

35. Joint venture – The two companies formed a joint venture to enter a new market.

36. Lending rate – Changes in the lending rate can impact borrowing costs for businesses.

37. Merger – The merger of two companies created a powerful new competitor in the market.

38. Net income – Net income is the company's total earnings after expenses have been deducted.

39. Overhead – Managing overhead costs is essential for maintaining profitability.

40. Portfolio – Diversifying your investment portfolio can help spread risk.

41. Recession – A recession can lead to decreased consumer spending and lower business investment.

42. Stock market – The stock market experienced a sharp decline in response to economic uncertainty.

43. Trade deficit – A trade deficit occurs when a country imports more goods than it exports.

44. Upsell – Salespeople often try to upsell customers on additional products or services.

45. Volatility – Stock markets can experience high levels of volatility during uncertain times.

46. Asset allocation – Proper asset allocation is key to achieving a balanced investment portfolio.

47. Balance sheet – The balance sheet provides a snapshot of a company's financial health.

48. Credit rating – A good credit rating can help businesses secure favorable terms on loans.

49. Due diligence – Conducting due diligence is essential before entering into any business agreement.

50. Exchange rate – Fluctuations in exchange rates can impact the profitability of international business transactions.

www.ingramcontent.com/pod-product-compliance
Lightning Source LLC
LaVergne TN
LVHW020442070526
838199LV00063B/4822